# ENGLISH
# PAPER PIECING
# WORKSHOP

18 EPP projects for beginners and beyond

Jenny Jackson

DAVID & CHARLES

www.davidandcharles.com

# CONTENTS

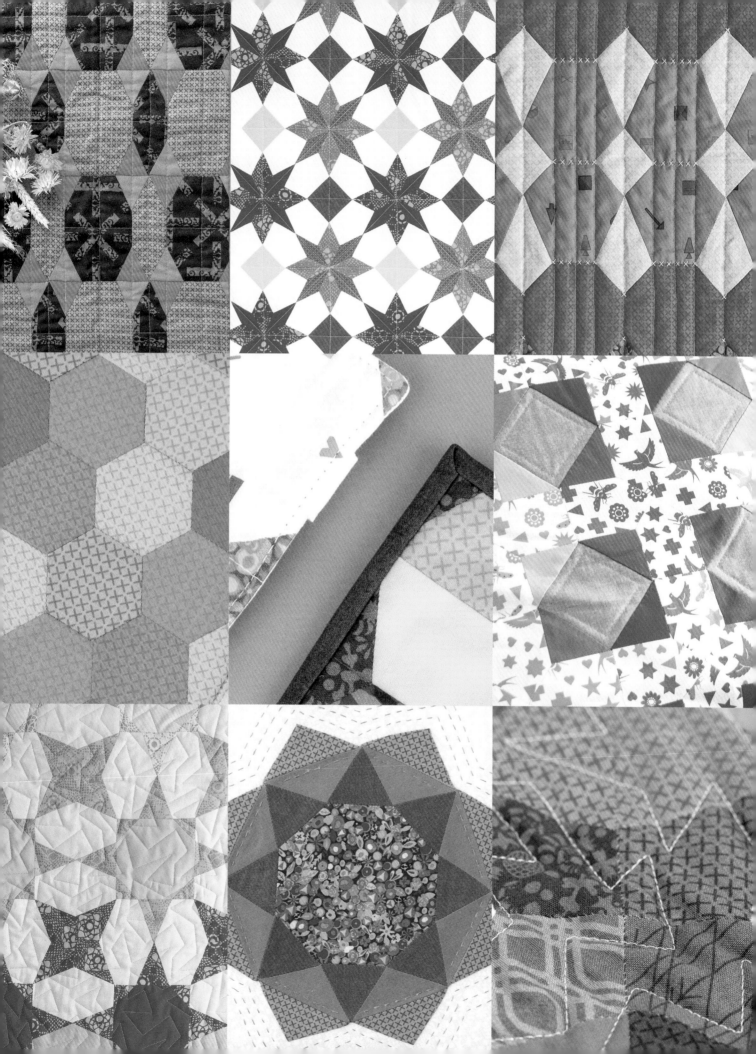

# FOREWORD

I am delighted to see Jenny Jackson's skilful use of the vibrant colors found in my work throughout the many distinctive projects she has created in this book. It's a real honor that she has chosen to use so many of my fabric designs.

*English Paper Piecing Workshop* is a study in the effective use of color and shape which is sure to bring inspiration and enjoyment to all readers. Thank you, Jenny, for bringing this project to life!

*alison glass*

# INTRODUCTION

Hands up if you love hand sewing? If you do, this is the book for you! English Paper Piecing (EPP) is my passion. It is so relaxing and creative as well. At the end of the day there is nothing better than snuggling up on the sofa with a favourite television programme and my latest EPP project and just chilling out. EPP is also portable. I always have a pouch with some basted shapes, my thread and scissors inside, good to go. You can catch me sewing on the beach, in a park or even on a train.

When it came to choosing a theme, immediately I thought of homeware. This is because I love having gorgeous handmade quilted projects on show in every room of my home - who doesn't like to be surrounded by pretty things?

Traditionally, hexagons are ubiquitous in EPP, but I have used a wide variety of shapes, both large and small. Many happy hours have been spent playing with different shapes to come up with eighteen geometric, modern makes for your home. Through colour and fabric placements, often secondary patterns can be created, too, so you can add a personal twist to the designs. The projects range from full-size quilts, to wall hangings, cushions and table settings. So if this technique is new to you, why not start off with a smaller item to find your EPP feet?

I love bold, bright fabrics, but all of the projects will look equally great in different palettes and styles. To help you visualise what your chosen scheme will look like, I have included a colouring layout with each project which you can photocopy and colour in at your leisure before cutting into your precious fabrics.

So get set and enjoy EPP'ing, wherever you may be - and, most importantly, experiment and have fun!

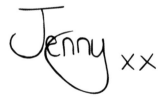

# TOOLS AND MATERIALS

## CUTTING TOOLS

### Rotary cutter
Rotary cutters are perfect for cutting accurate straight lines. They are very sharp and can cut through a few layers of fabric with one cut. They must be used with quilting rulers and a cutting mat.

### Quilting rulers
Acrylic quilting rulers are vital when using a rotary cutter. They come in a wide variety of sizes. I use larger ones for cutting out bigger pieces of fabric and smaller ones for cutting ¼in all around my paper templates. My favourites are by Creative Grids as they are non-slip and have really useful measurement markings on them.

### Cutting mat
You must use a self-healing cutting mat when using a rotary cutter. Large mats (e.g. 24 x 36in [61 x 91cm]) are most useful. The grid lines are handy, but use the measurements on your ruler when cutting out as these are more accurate.

### Fabric scissors
These large scissors are perfect for cutting through wadding and trimming fabric. They can also be used instead of a rotary cutter for cutting out fabrics.

### Embroidery scissors
These small, sharp scissors are ideal for cutting threads, snipping off corners and for any delicate cutting that needs to be done.

## BASTING TOOLS

### Fabric glue pen and refills
Fabric glue pens are used to baste the fabric pieces to the paper templates. They are quick and easy to use, and this method produces crisp edges. Sewline is my go-to brand as the glue does not leave any sticky residue on the fabric and the paper templates are easy to remove, no matter how long the pieces have been left basted – they are also simple to refill.

### Quilt basting spray
This spray is a super-fast way of basting when making your quilt sandwich, or just for basting the quilt top to the wadding. My favourite is 505 Temporary Adhesive for Fabric as it holds really well, so the layers don't shift when quilting.

## SEWING TOOLS

### Needles
I use a size 11 Milliners (also known as Straw) needle for all my English Paper Piecing. They are long and very sharp and, as they are thin, they don't leave holes in the fabric.

### Pins
My go-to are flat-headed pins. I find them the easiest to push through the fabric and wadding, and they are excellent for holding everything in place when sewing straight or curved seams.

### Quilting clips
These small clips are superb for holding binding in place as they easily secure several layers. I also use them for holding larger EPP shapes together when hand-sewing as they prevent the shapes from moving out of alignment.

# FABRICS, THREADS
# AND WADDING

*Note: The projects in this book assume a minimum usable width of fabric of 42in (107cm).*

## Fabrics

Quilting-weight cotton has been used for all of the projects in this book. It is ideal for quilt tops, linings and backings. Using good-quality fabric really does make all the difference for amazing looking projects. It can be bought off-the-bolt or in fat quarters or fat eighths. Some fabric ranges have extra-wide widths especially for backings, which saves you having to join pieces.

## Threads

I have used a variety of different high-quality threads throughout the book. I use 80-weight cotton threads for joining EPP shapes and for appliqué, 50-weight cotton for machine piecing and quilting, and cotton floss for embroidery and hand quilting. My go-to are Aurifil threads as they come in different weights and are available in a wide range of colours.

## Wadding

Wadding is the layer between your quilt top and backing. It comes in different materials and lofts (thicknesses). My favourite is Sew Simple's Super-soft Light 80/20 Blend wadding, a mixture of 80% cotton with 20% polyester, which can be used for hand or machine quilting. For items such as potholders that require a heat-resistant layer for safety, use insulated wadding. I like to use Sew Simple's Insulating Wadding.

# HOW TO EPP

## CUTTING AND BASTING

1   Press your fabric so it is free from creases. Sometimes, especially if you are cutting several of the same template, it is more efficient to cut your fabric into strips. These strips need to be ½in higher than the template you will be cutting out (i.e. ¼in seam allowance top and bottom).

2   Place the fabric wrong side up on your cutting mat. Place your template on top of the fabric.

3   Mark a ¼in seam allowance all around the template. You can do this using the ¼in line on a quilting ruler.

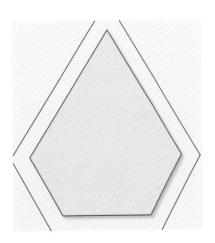

**TIP**

*If you are using a directional print or fussy cutting (i.e. selecting the print motif you want in a particular shape), make sure the template is in the correct orientation. You may need more fabric than given in the requirements with the project for this.*

4   Turn your template 180 degrees and place it ¼in away from the line you have just marked.

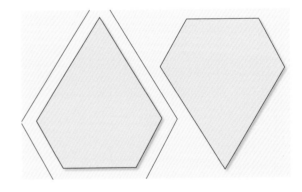

5   Mark a ¼in seam allowance all around the template as you did in Step 3.

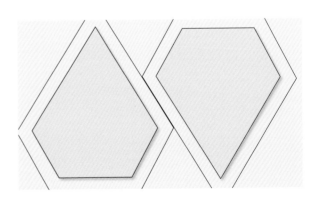

**6** Continue in the same manner until you get to the end of the strip, or have marked the number of shapes required.

**7** Cut along the marked lines using a rotary cutter and quilting ruler, or use a pair of fabric scissors.

**8** Take a paper template and a corresponding fabric shape. Place the fabric shape on a clean, flat surface with the wrong side facing upwards. Centre the paper template on top.

**9** Using a glue pen, lightly glide your pen across the fabric just beyond the edge of the paper template. If you prefer, you can glue around the edge of the paper template instead. There is no right or wrong, so use whichever method works best for you.

**10** Fold one edge of the fabric over onto the template and finger press to stick the seam allowance in place.

**11** Working either clockwise or anticlockwise, work your way around the template in the same manner until the shape is fully basted.

**12** Sometimes 'dog-ears' will be formed at the points of the shape. Do not cut these off as they will be hidden when you join shapes or will be 'lost' when squaring-up a quilt after quilting, or for appliquéd EPP units they can be tucked under when stitching the EPP unit in place.

*'Dog-ear'*

## TIP

*If you prefer, you can hand-baste templates in place using long tacking stitches. Whether gluing or tacking, try to baste all of the shapes in the same direction as any 'dog-ears' will then also be facing the same way. When the shapes are joined the 'dog-ears' will then nest neatly, giving a flatter finish.*

# SEWING SHAPES AND BLOCKS TOGETHER

**13** Once you have basted your shapes it is time to get sewing! Place the shapes you are sewing together right sides together, taking care to match up accurately the edges you will be joining. Knot the end of your thread and then, starting at one end of the seam, insert the needle through the folds of both edges, catching just a few threads – you are not stitching through the paper template.

**14** Oversew along the length of the seam with tiny whipstitches – catch just a few threads and don't stitch through the paper template. Your stitches should be small enough not to show on the right side.

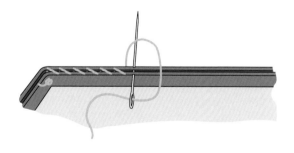

## TIP

*Once all the sides of a shape have been joined to other shapes, you can remove the paper template. This makes things lighter and easier to handle, and you can re-use the templates multiple times.*

**15** When you get to the end of the seam, knot off the thread.

**16** Open out the shapes.

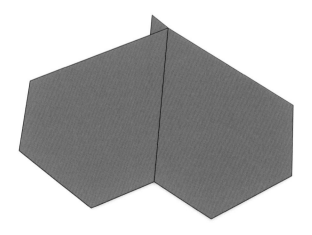

**17** To add another shape, repeat Steps 13–16.

**18** To sew blocks together, follow the method described in Steps 13–17.

# APPLIQUÉING EPP UNITS IN PLACE

**19** Making sure the edges of the EPP unit are neat and crisp is the key to having a fantastic-looking appliquéd block. My tip is to press the edge blocks, wait for them to cool down and then carefully remove the paper templates, and then press again, taking your time to make sure the seam allowances are neatly tucked under.

**20** Place the background fabric right side up and pin the EPP unit in place on top.

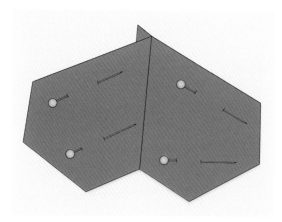

**21** Knot the end of your thread and then come up from the back of the fabric and catch a few threads of the EPP unit's edge.

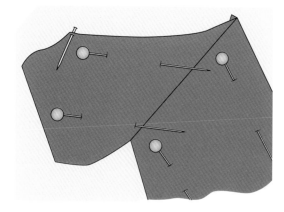

**22** Sew all the way around the outer edge of the EPP unit in this way using a small whipstitch. Use small stitches and keep them close together as then the stitching is almost invisible.

**23** When you get to a 'dog-ear', finish with your needle on the right side of the EPP unit.

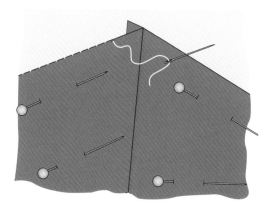

**24** Fold the 'dog-ear' neatly underneath the EPP unit. I often use a blunt pair of scissors to push the 'dog-ear' under.

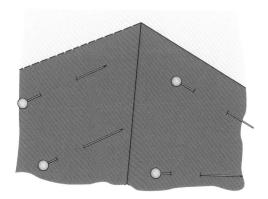

**25** Carry on sewing around the EPP unit in the same manner until it has been completely stitched in place.

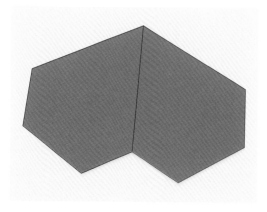

# PROJECTS

Whether you love large projects or prefer smaller makes, there is plenty to choose from. All use the time-tested technique of English Paper Piecing, but the designs have been given a modern makeover. So dive in and enjoy!

*The projects in this book assume a minimum usable width of fabric of 42in (107cm). Dimensions are given height x width.*

# SPINNING SPECTRUM

Have fun playing with the colour spectrum in this bright, fun quilt. Combined with low-volume whites and creams, and stylish greys, the spinning spectrum blocks really sing!

**Approximate size: 57½in (146cm) square**

## FABRIC REQUIREMENTS

- One fat eighth each of eight different tones (light to dark) of pinks/purples
- One fat eighth each of eight different tones (light to dark) of yellows/oranges/reds
- One fat eighth each of eight different tones (light to dark) of blues
- One fat eighth each of eight different tones (light to dark) of greens
- ½yd (50cm) each of five different whites/creams low-volume solids and/or prints
- ⅝yd (60cm) each of four different grey prints
- 66in (166cm) square of backing fabric
- ½yd (50cm) of binding fabric
- 66in (166cm) square of wadding

## TEMPLATES

- Three hundred and twenty-eight Template A
- Eighty Template B
- Two hundred and eighty-eight Template C
- Thirty-six Template D
- Thirty-six Template E

## TIPS

*For details about cutting and preparing shapes for EPP, see **How to EPP, Cutting and basting**.*

*If you like a narrower and tighter binding, cut your binding strips 2¼in wide (instead of 2½in wide).*

# CUTTING

## Pinks/purples

· Eleven Template A from each tone

## Yellows/oranges/reds

· Ten Template A from each tone

## Blues

· Ten Template A from each tone

## Greens

· Ten Template A from each tone

## Whites/creams

· Eighty Template B – you could cut sixteen from each fabric, or more from some fabrics and fewer from others

## Greys

· Seventy-two Template C from each fabric
· Nine Template D from each fabric
· Nine Template E from each fabric

## Binding fabric

· Seven 2½in wide strips across the width of the fabric

# SPECTRUM BLOCKS

1   Take one Template A of each pinks/purples tone (i.e. eight in total). Working in a clockwise direction, arrange them from lightest to darkest as shown.

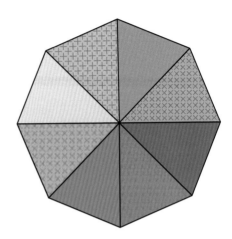

2   Sew them together to make one pinks/purples spectrum block.

3   Working as described in Steps 1 and 2, make the following:

· Eleven pinks/purples spectrum blocks

· Ten yellows/oranges/red spectrum blocks

· Ten blues spectrum blocks

· Ten greens spectrum blocks

You will have forty-one spectrum blocks in total.

## TIP

*For details about sewing shapes and blocks together, see* **How to EPP, Sewing shapes and blocks together**.

## LOW-VOLUME BLOCKS

**4**  Take two different white/cream Template B and sew them together on their long straight edge as shown to make one low-volume block.

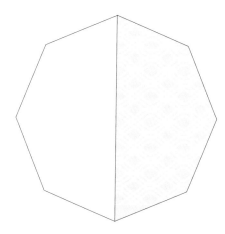

**5**  Mixing and matching, and using two different whites/creams each time, repeat Step 4 to make a total of forty low-volume blocks.

## STAR BLOCKS

**6**  Take four different grey Template C and sew them together on their short edge as shown to make one star block.

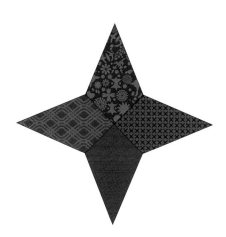

**7**  Repeat Step 6 to make a total of sixty-four star blocks.

## EDGE BLOCKS

**8**  Take one grey Template C, one grey Template D and one grey Template E, each one a different grey print.

**9**  Arrange as shown and sew them together on their short edge to make one edge block.

**10**  Repeat Steps 8 and 9 to make a total of thirty-two edge blocks.

## CORNER BLOCKS

**11**  Take one grey Template D and one grey Template E, each one a different grey print.

**12**  Arrange as shown and sew them together on their short edge to make one corner block.

**13**  Repeat Steps 11 and 12 to make a total of four corner blocks.

## QUILT LAYOUT

*Follow the layout diagram when constructing the quilt top.*

**14** Arrange the blocks as shown, taking care to orientate the spectrum and low-volume blocks as indicated.

**15** Sew the blocks together. To make the quilt top easier to handle, you can sew the blocks into rows and then sew the rows together.

**16** Once the quilt top is complete, remove all remaining paper pieces and then press.

## QUILTING AND FINISHING

**17** Make a quilt sandwich of the quilt top, the wadding and the backing fabric. See **Quilt Techniques, Making a quilt sandwich**.

**18** Quilt as desired. Mine was quilted with an all-over jagged straight-line pattern. See **Quilt Techniques, Quilting**.

**19** Square-up and bind to finish. See **Quilt Techniques, Squaring-up** and **Quilt Techniques, Binding**.

## COLOURING LAYOUT

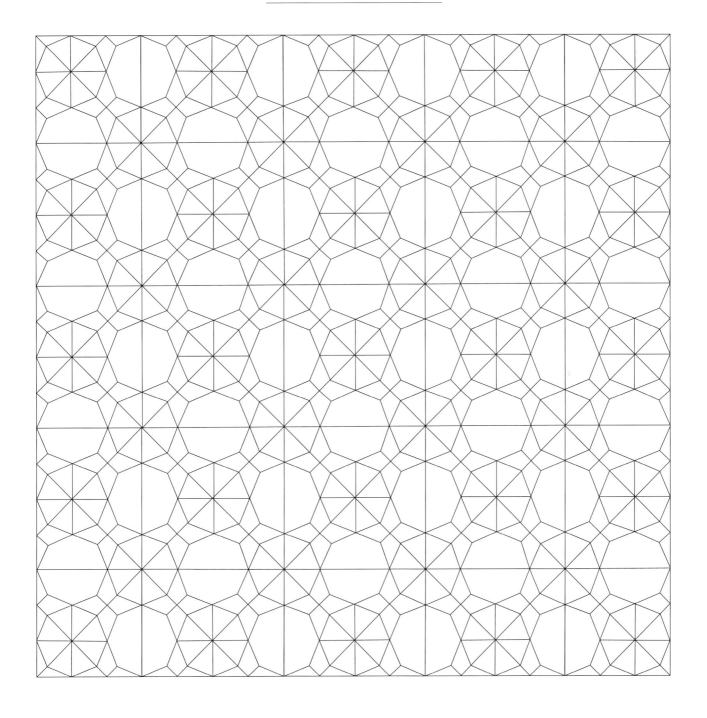

# GEMSTONE LAMPSHADE

Whether used as a lamp or ceiling shade, this hand-sewn EPP lampshade will add a classy and unique touch to your home.

**Approximate size: 13¼in (33.5cm) high x 11¾in (30cm) diameter**

## FABRIC REQUIREMENTS

· ½yd (50cm) of turquoise novelty print
· ⅜yd (40cm) of dark blue tone-on-tone
· One fat quarter of turquoise tone-on-tone

## OTHER REQUIREMENTS

· One 12⅞ x 38in (32.5 x 96.5cm) rectangle of self-adhesive lampshade backing material
· 11¾in (30cm) diameter circular lampshade frame (two rings, a top and bottom ring)
· A roll of ⅞in (21mm)-wide double-sided sticky tape
· A roll of ½in (12mm)-wide double-sided sticky tape
· Pegs
· Blunt knife

## TEMPLATES

· Twenty-nine Template A
· Thirty-eight Template B
· Eighteen Template C
· Two Template D
· Four Template E
· Four Template F

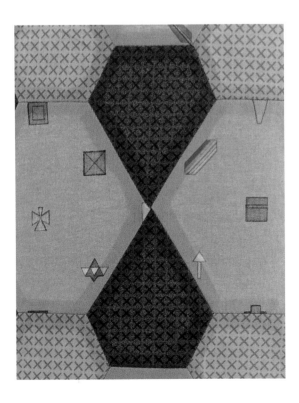

## TIP

*For details about cutting and preparing shapes for EPP, see **How to EPP, Cutting and basting**.*

## CUTTING

### Turquoise novelty print

· Twenty-nine Template A
· Two Template D

### Dark blue tone-on-tone

· Twenty Template B
· Eighteen Template C
· Four Template F

### Turquoise tone-on-tone

· Eighteen Template B
· Four Template E

## EPP PANEL

*Follow the layout diagram when constructing the EPP panel.*

1   Sew the prepared shapes together as shown to make the EPP panel.

2   Press the panel and then remove all remaining paper pieces.

3   Press again, but this time press the seam allowance open on both long edges of the panel. Keep the seam allowance on the shorter edges turned in.

## TIP

*For details about sewing shapes and blocks together, see* **How to EPP, Sewing shapes and blocks together**.

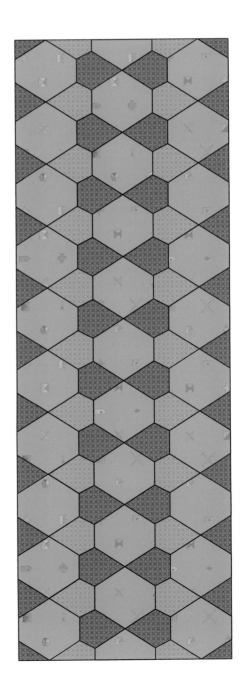

# CONSTRUCTING THE LAMPSHADE

**4** Place the EPP panel wrong side up on a clean, flat surface.

**5** Release-paper side down, place the self-adhesive lampshade backing material on top of the EPP panel as shown. The left-hand short edge of the backing material should align with the left-hand edge of the EPP panel, leaving excess EPP panel showing at the right-hand edge. Leave the same amount of EPP panel showing top and bottom.

**6** Little by little, remove the release paper, smoothing and sticking the backing in place as you go.

**7** Down the full length of the short edge of the backing material on the side where the EPP panel is showing, stick a piece of ⅞in-wide double-sided sticky tape, placing it approximately ½in in from the edge of the backing material as shown.

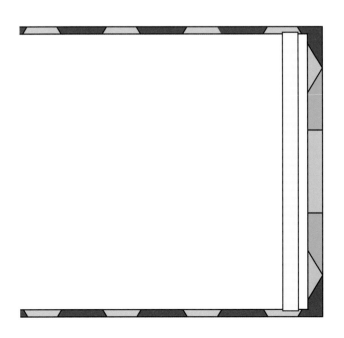

**8** Peel off the tape's backing. Making sure the seam allowance stays turned in, fold the EPP panel over onto the tape and stick it in place to create a neatened short edge. Place to one side.

**9** Take one of the lampshade rings and the ½in-wide double-sided sticky tape. Attach tape all the way around the ring. Remove the backing and as you do so 'pinch' the tape over the ring so that it is entirely covered. Repeat for the other ring.

**10** Place the top lampshade ring on the EPP panel at its un-neatened short end, just above the top of the lampshade backing material, and peg in place as shown. At the same end, place the bottom lampshade ring on the EPP panel, just below the bottom of the lampshade backing material, and peg in place as shown.

**11** Hold both rings and roll them along the fabric, stopping approximately 5in before you get to the neatened short edge. Place a piece of ⅞in-wide double-sided sticky tape on top of the fabric of the neatened short edge as shown. The outer long edge of the tape should align with the outer edge of the fabric. The top and bottom of the tape should align with the top and bottom of the lampshade backing material. Peel off the tape's backing.

**12** Remove the pegs from the rings and keep rolling the lampshade so it sticks to the tape placed on the fabric in Step 11. To secure, finger press along the length of the tape from the inside of the lampshade.

**13** Starting with the bottom lampshade ring, fold the excess fabric over the ring as shown. Using a blunt knife, push the fabric underneath the ring, which will keep it well tucked in. When tucking in the fabric where the lampshade fabric overlaps, if it's too bulky then trim off the inside fabric.

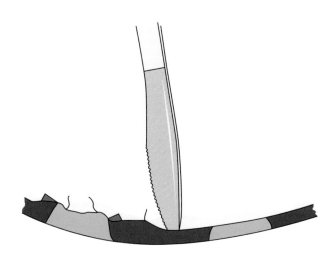

**14** Repeat Step 13 with the top lampshade ring. Where the spokes are, carefully snip into the fabric so it can be manipulated around the spokes and tucked in neatly.

## TIP

*Choose fabrics that complement your décor to create a stunning bespoke lampshade for your living space.*

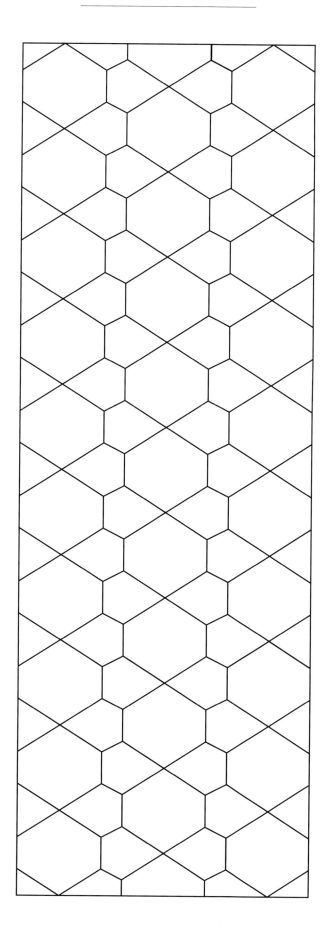

# SALT AND PEPPER

Add a modern vibe to your table setting with this funky runner. Why not choose hues that will pack a punch with your home décor scheme and really make a statement?

**Approximate size: 12 x 48½in (30.5 x 123cm)**

## FABRIC REQUIREMENTS

- ½yd (50cm) of grey
- ⅜yd (40cm) of dark grey/black
- One fat quarter of blue
- One fat quarter of pink
- ⅜yd (40cm) of binding fabric
- 16 x 53in (40.5 x 135cm) of backing fabric
- 16 x 53in (40.5 x 135cm) of wadding

## TEMPLATES

- Thirty-three Template A
- Twenty-two Template B
- Eighty-eight Template C
- Forty-four Template D

## TIPS

*If you would like to use one of the triangle fabrics for your binding as I have, you will need ⅝yd (60cm) of that fabric in total.*

*For details about cutting and preparing shapes for EPP, see* **How to EPP, Cutting and basting**.

*If you like a narrower and tighter binding, cut your binding strips 2¼in wide (instead of 2½in wide).*

## CUTTING

### Grey
· Eighteen Template A
· Ten Template B

### Dark grey/black
· Fifteen Template A
· Twelve Template B

### Blue
· Forty-four Template C
· Twenty-two Template D

### Pink
· Forty-four Template C
· Twenty-two Template D

### Binding fabric
· Four 2½in wide strips across the width of the fabric

## TIP

*For details about sewing shapes together, see* **How to EPP, Sewing shapes and blocks together**.

## GREY BLOCKS

1   Take three grey Template A, two dark grey/black Template B, four blue Template C, four pink Template C, two blue Template D and two pink Template D.

2   Arrange as shown and sew together to make one grey block.

3   Repeat Steps 1 and 2 to make a total of six grey blocks.

## DARK GREY/BLACK BLOCKS

4   Take three dark grey/black Template A, two grey Template B, four blue Template C, four pink Template C, two blue Template D and two pink Template D.

5   Arrange as shown and sew together to make one dark grey/black block.

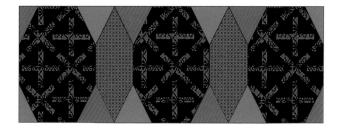

6   Repeat Steps 4 and 5 to make a total of five dark grey/black blocks.

# TABLE RUNNER LAYOUT

*Follow the layout diagram when constructing the table runner top.*

7 Arrange the grey blocks and dark grey/black blocks as shown, taking care to alternate them as indicated.

8 Sew the blocks together.

9 Once the table runner top is sewn together, remove all remaining paper pieces and then press.

## QUILTING AND FINISHING

**10** Make a quilt sandwich of the table runner top, the wadding and the backing fabric. See **Quilt Techniques, Making a quilt sandwich**.

**11** Quilt as desired. Mine was quilted in a simple grid pattern using two different thread colours to match the blue and pink triangles. See **Quilt Techniques, Quilting**.

**12** Square-up and bind to finish. See **Quilt Techniques, Squaring-up** and **Quilt Techniques, Binding**.

## TIP

*To complete your table setting, you could use the runner templates to create matching placemats and coasters.*

## COLOURING LAYOUT

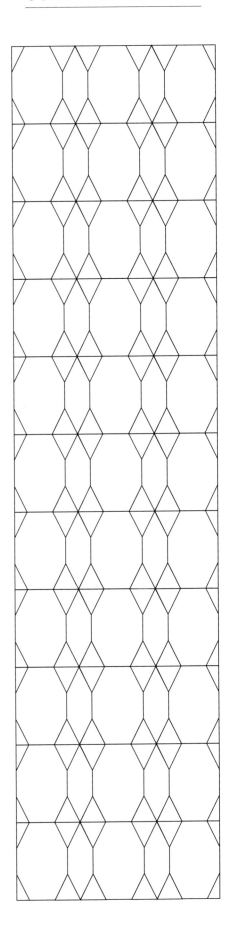

# STAR BRIGHT

Calm colours combined with a graphic design make this the perfect wall hanging to add a touch of serenity to any room in your home.

**Approximate size: 33¾ x 24¾in (86 x 63cm), excluding tabs**

## FABRIC REQUIREMENTS

- One fat eighth of aqua
- One fat eighth of dark purple
- One fat quarter of blue print
- One fat quarter of blue tone-on-tone or solid
- One fat quarter of purple print
- One fat quarter of purple tone-on-tone or solid
- 1¾yd (1.6m) of white for background, hanging tabs and binding
- 38 x 29in (96.5 x 73cm) of backing fabric
- 38 x 29in (96.5 x 73cm) of wadding

## TEMPLATES

- Thirty-one Template A
- Ninety-six Template B
- Eighty-two Template C
- Ninety-six Template D

## TIPS

*If you would like to use a contrasting fabric for the hanging tabs and binding, you will need 1¼yd (1.1m) of white background fabric and ½yd (50cm) of hanging tabs and binding fabric.*

*For details about cutting and preparing shapes for EPP, see **How to EPP, Cutting and basting**.*

*If you like a narrower and tighter binding, cut your binding strips 2¼in wide (instead of 2½in wide).*

## CUTTING

### Aqua

· Nine Template A

### Dark purple

· Eight Template A

### Blue print

· Forty-eight Template C

### Blue tone-on-tone or solid

· Forty-eight Template D

### Purple print

· Twenty-four Template C

### Purple tone-on-tone or solid

· Twenty-four Template D

### White

· Fourteen Template A
· Ninety-six Template B
· Ten Template C
· Twenty-four Template D
· Three 4 x 6in rectangles for hanging tabs
· Four 2½in wide strips across the width of the
  fabric for binding

## TIP

*For details about sewing shapes and blocks
together, see* **How to EPP, Sewing shapes
and blocks together**.

## STAR BLOCKS

1  Take four blue print Template C and four blue tone-
   on-tone or solid Template D. Arrange as shown and
   sew them together to make one blue star block.

2  Repeat Step 1 to make a total of twelve blue star
   blocks.

3  Take four purple print Template C and four purple
   tone-on-tone or solid Template D. Arrange as shown
   and sew them together to make one purple star
   block.

4  Repeat Step 3 to make a total of six purple star
   blocks.

# BACKGROUND BLOCKS

**5**   Take one aqua Template A and four white Template B. Arrange as shown and sew them together to make one aqua background block.

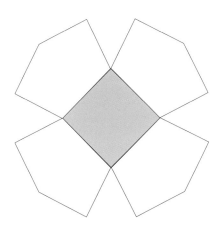

**6**   Repeat Step 5 to make a total of nine aqua background blocks.

**7**   Take one dark purple Template A and four white Template B. Arrange as shown and sew them together to make one dark purple background block.

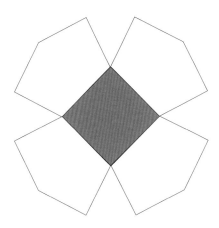

**8**   Repeat Step 7 to make a total of eight dark purple background blocks.

# A/B EDGE BLOCKS

**9**   Take one white Template A and two white Template B. Arrange as shown and sew them together to make one A/B edge block.

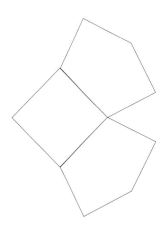

**10**   Repeat Step 9 to make a total of fourteen A/B edge blocks.

# C/D EDGE BLOCKS

**11**   Take one white Template C and two white Template D. Arrange as shown and sew them together to make one C/D edge block.

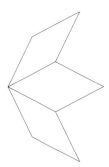

**12**   Repeat Step 11 to make a total of ten C/D edge blocks.

**13**   You will have four white Template D left over. These will be added to the corners of the hanging in Step 19.

# QUILT LAYOUT

**14** Take three blue star blocks and two dark purple background blocks. Arrange as shown and sew them together to make one odd-numbered row.

**15** Repeat Step 14 to make a total of four odd-numbered rows (Rows 1, 3, 5 and 7).

**16** Take two purple star blocks and three aqua background blocks. Arrange as shown and sew them together to make one even-numbered row.

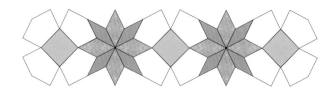

**17** Repeat Step 16 to make a total of three even-numbered rows (Rows 2, 4 and 6).

**18** Starting with Row 1 at the top and ending with Row 7 at the bottom, join the rows together as shown to create the quilt centre.

**19** Sew the A/B and C/D edge blocks to the quilt centre. It is easier to handle the quilt if they are added one by one. Sew a white Template D to each corner.

**20** Remove all remaining paper pieces and then press.

## TIP

*If you love this design, you could use the repeat pattern to create a larger quilt. All you need is more fabric and templates!*

# HANGING TABS

**21** Take one 4 x 6in white rectangle. On each long edge, turn over a ¼in seam to the wrong side and press. Wrong sides together, fold the strip in half lengthwise, so the neatened long edges match up, and press. Topstitch approximately ⅛in in from each long edge using a longer stitch length than usual.

**22** Repeat Step 21 with your two remaining 4 x 6in white rectangles.

**23** Fold each strip in half so the raw edges match up. These will form your hanging tabs when attached to the quilt.

# QUILTING AND FINISHING

**24** Make a quilt sandwich of the quilt top, the wadding and the backing fabric. See **Quilt Techniques, Making a quilt sandwich**.

**25** Quilt as desired. Using thread to match the white background, mine was straight-line quilted horizontally and vertically though the centre of the Template A shapes to create a square grid. Diagonal lines were then stitched across the quilt going through the centres of star blocks and the corners of the stitched squares. See **Quilt Techniques, Quilting**.

**26** Square-up the quilt as shown. It should measure 33¾ x 24¾in.

**27** Place the quilt on a clean, flat surface with the backing fabric facing upwards. Take one hanging tab and place it in the centre of the top edge of the quilt, matching up the raw edges of the tab with the raw edges of the quilt. Pin in place. In the same way, position another tab so its outer edge is 2¾in in from the right-hand side of the quilt, and the remaining tab so its outer edge is 2¾in in from the left-hand side of the quilt.

**28** Prepare your binding. See **Quilt Techniques, Binding**. Machine stitch your binding to the back of the quilt (not to the front). This will trap the hanging tabs in the seam so they are securely attached. Fold the binding over to the front of the quilt and neatly hand-stitch in place.

## COLOURING LAYOUT

# CUPCAKE FRINGE

Add a pop of colour to any wall in your home with this quick-to-make groovy hanging. The fringe gives a fun and funky touch!

**Approximate size: 19 x 12½in (48 x 32cm), excluding tabs and fringe**

## FABRIC REQUIREMENTS

- One fat eighth of deep pink solid or tone-on-tone
- One fat eighth of pink/coral print
- One fat eighth of white print
- One fat quarter of pink floral print
- One fat eighth of white solid or tone-on-tone
- ½yd (50cm) of white for backing and hanging tabs
- 25 x 20in (63.5 x 51cm) of wadding
- Embroidery floss for hand-quilted decoration, optional
- 21yd (20m) of macramé cord
- Washi tape or similar

## TEMPLATES

- Eight Template A
- Sixteen Template B
- Twenty Template C
- Fifteen Template D

## TIP

*For details about cutting and preparing shapes for EPP, see* **How to EPP, Cutting and basting**.

## CUTTING

### Deep pink

· Eight Template A

### Pink/coral print

· Eight Template B

### White print

· Eight Template B

### Pink floral print

· Ten Template C
· Ten Template D

### White solid or tone-on-tone

· Ten Template C
· Five Template D

### White

· One 19½ x 13in rectangle
· Three 2½ x 5in rectangles

## WALL HANGING FRONT

**1**   Take four white print Template B, five pink floral Template C and five pink floral Template D. Arrange as shown and sew together.

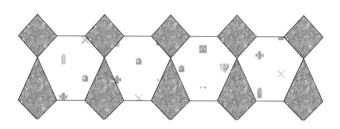

**2**   Take four deep pink Template A and five white solid/tone-on-tone Template C and sew them to the bottom of the unit made in Step 1.

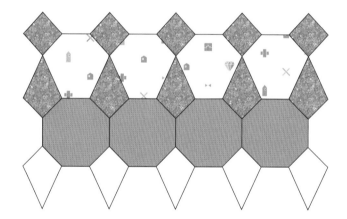

## TIP

*For details about sewing shapes and blocks together, see* **How to EPP, Sewing shapes and blocks together**.

**3** Take four pink/coral print Template B and five white solid/tone-on-tone Template D and sew them to the bottom of the unit made in Step 2.

**5** Take four deep pink Template A and five pink floral Template C and sew them to the bottom of the unit made in Step 4.

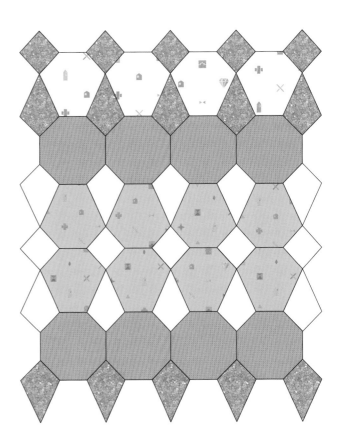

**4** Take four pink/coral print Template B and five white solid/tone-on-tone Template C and sew them to the bottom of the unit made in Step 3.

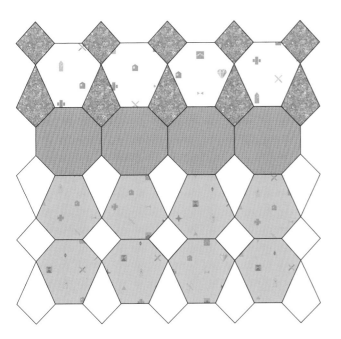

**6** Take four white print Template B and five pink floral Template D and sew them to the bottom of the unit made in Step 5.

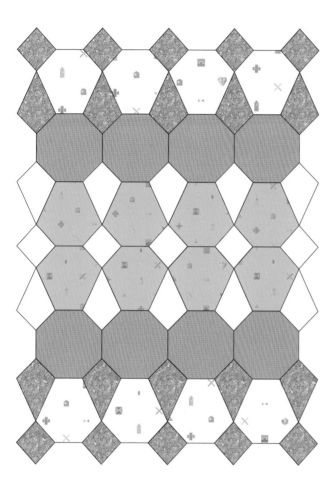

**7** Once the wall hanging top is complete, remove all remaining paper pieces and then press.

## QUILTING

**8** Baste the wall hanging top to the wadding.

**9** Quilt as desired. Mine was straight-line machine quilted with evenly-spaced vertical lines. Using embroidery floss, I then hand-quilted some cross stitches along some of the seams and seam junctions for extra decoration. See **Quilt Techniques, Quilting**.

**10** Trimming evenly all around, trim the wall hanging so it measures 19½ x 13in. Put to one side.

## HANGING TABS

**11** Take one 2½ x 5in white rectangle. On each long edge, turn over a ¼in seam to the wrong side and press. Wrong sides together, fold the strip in half lengthwise, so the neatened long edges match up, and press. Topstitch approximately ⅛in in from each long edge using a longer stitch length than usual.

**12** Repeat Step 11 with your two remaining 2½ x 5in white rectangles.

**13** Fold each strip in half so the raw edges match up. These will form your hanging tabs when attached to the wall hanging.

## FINISHING

**14** Cut 8in lengths from the macramé cord. You should have approximately one hundred lengths in total.

**15** Place the quilted wall hanging on a clean, flat surface with the right side facing upwards. Place the lengths of macramé cord evenly along the hanging's bottom edge as shown. Note: leave ¼in at each side of the hanging without cord. Hold the ends of the cords in place with washi tape. (Washi tape is easy to remove and won't damage the cords.)

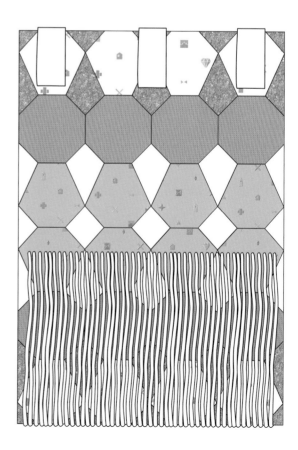

## COLOURING LAYOUT

16  Now take one hanging tab and place it in the centre of the top edge of the hanging, matching up the raw edges of the tab with the raw edges of the hanging as shown. Pin in place. In the same way, position another tab so its outer edge is 1½in in from the right-hand side of the hanging, and the remaining tab so it is 1½in in from the left-hand side of the hanging.

17  Right sides together, place the white 19½ x 13in rectangle on top of the wall hanging. Pin or clip in place, taking care not to trap any of the cords in the seam allowance.

18  Sew all the way around using a ¼in seam allowance, leaving an approximately 4in gap for turning on one long edge.

19  Clip the corners to reduce bulk, taking care not to snip into the stitching.

20  Turn right side out through the gap. Carefully poke the corners out and then press carefully to give crisp edges, making sure the seam allowance is neatly tucked under inside the gap.

21  Topstitch all the way around the hanging, approximately ⅛in in from the edge, with a longer stitch length than usual (I used the same length stitch I that I used for my quilting). This will close the turning gap.

22  Place the wall hanging on a clean, flat surface, straighten out all of the cords to form a fringe and then trim to neaten. You can trim the cords so they are all the same length to give straight fringe or trim them at an angle as I did to make a lower point in the centre of the fringe.

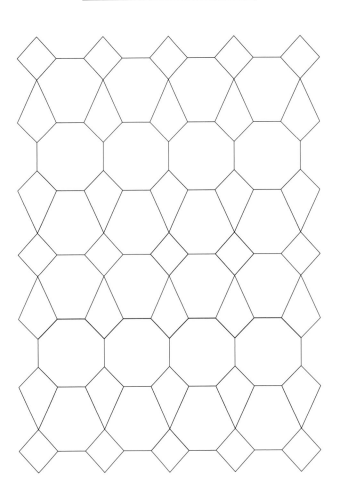

## TIPS

*In Step 18, take a few backstitches at the start and end of your stitching.*

*In Step 21, sew a double line of stitching along the top and bottom edges to secure the hanging tabs and cords in place.*

# CELTIC KNOTS

This fun block combines EPP and appliqué to create a Celtic knot effect. Placing each colourway on the diagonal gives a lovely subtle colourwash running over the quilt's surface.

**Approximate size: 54in (137cm) square**

## FABRIC REQUIREMENTS

· ⅞yd (80cm) each of three different low-volume or solid cream/white
· Light blue: two different fat eighths, one solid/tone-on-tone/print and one solid/tone-on-tone
· Mid blue: one fat quarter solid/tone-on-tone/print and one fat eighth solid/tone-on-tone
· Dark blue: ⅜yd (40cm) solid/tone-on-tone/print and one fat eighth solid/tone-on-tone
· Turquoise: ½yd (50cm) solid/tone-on-tone/print and one fat quarter solid/tone-on-tone
· Light turquoise: ⅜yd (40cm) solid/tone-on-tone/print and one fat eighth solid/tone-on-tone
· Light green: one fat quarter solid/tone-on-tone/print and one fat eighth solid/tone-on-tone
· Mid green: two different fat eighths, one solid/tone-on-tone/print and one solid/tone-on-tone
· 62in (157cm) square of backing fabric
· ½yd (50cm) of binding fabric
· 62in (157cm) square of wadding

## TEMPLATES

· One hundred and twenty-eight Template A
· Sixteen Template B
· Sixty-four Template C

## TIPS

*For details about cutting and preparing shapes for EPP, see* **How to EPP, Cutting and basting**.

*If you like a narrower and tighter binding, cut your binding strips 2¼in wide (instead of 2½in wide). In place of a single-fabric binding, why not use leftovers to make a scrappy binding? You need enough strips to make an approximate 226in (5.8m) length when joined.*

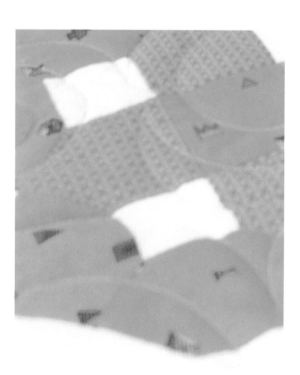

# CUTTING

## Cream/white
· From one fabric: Six 14in squares
· From two fabrics: Five 14in squares each

## Light blue
· Eight Template A and one Template B from the solid/tone-on-tone/print
· Four Template C from the solid/tone-on-tone

## Mid blue
· Sixteen Template A and two Template B from the solid/tone-on-tone/print
· Eight Template C from the solid/tone-on-tone

## Dark blue
· Twenty-four Template A and three Template B from the solid/tone-on-tone/print
· Twelve Template C from the solid/tone-on-tone

## Turquoise
· Thirty-two Template A and four Template B from the solid/tone-on-tone/print
· Sixteen Template C from the solid/tone-on-tone

## Light turquoise
· Twenty-four Template A and three Template B from the solid/tone-on-tone/print
· Twelve Template C from the solid/tone-on-tone

## Light green
· Sixteen Template A and two Template B from the solid/tone-on-tone/print
· Eight Template C from the solid/tone-on-tone

## Mid green
· Eight Template A and one Template B from the solid/tone-on-tone/print
· Four Template C from the solid/tone-on-tone

## Binding fabric
· Six 2½in wide strips across the width of the fabric

## TIPS

*Keep your Template A, B and C shapes for each colourway grouped together so everything is organised for when you start making the EPP rosettes.*

*For details about sewing shapes and blocks together, see* **How to EPP, Sewing shapes and blocks together**.

# EPP ROSETTES

1   Take the one light blue Template B and the four light blue Template C. Arrange as shown and sew together.

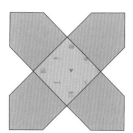

2   Take the eight light blue Template A and sew them to the unit made in Step 1 as shown. This completes one EPP rosette.

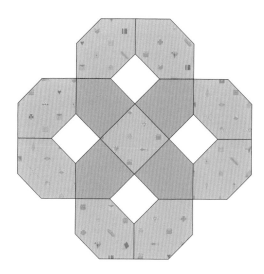

3   Working as described in Steps 1 and 2, make the following EPP rosettes:

· One light blue

· Two mid blue

· Three dark blue

· Four turquoise

· Three light turquoise

· Two light green

· One mid green

You will have sixteen EPP rosettes in total.

## TIPS

*For details about appliquéing the EPP rosettes to a background fabric, see* **How to EPP, Appliquéing EPP units in place**.

*When making the EPP blocks you may wish to mix and match the background squares for EPP rosettes of the same colourway.*

# EPP BLOCKS

4   Take one 14in cream/white square. Lightly fold it in half lengthways and finger press. Open out and then lightly fold it in half widthways and finger press. Open out. This is your background square.

5   Take the light blue EPP rosette. Press, remove all the paper pieces and then press again, making sure the outer seam allowance is neatly pressed under.

6   Place the background square right side up. Using the creased guidelines made in Step 4, right side up, position the EPP rosette centrally on top. Pin to secure.

7   Appliqué the EPP rosette in place around its outer edges and also around the inner square 'gaps'. Press. This is one EPP block.

8   Repeat Steps 4–7 with your remaining 14in low-volume or solid cream/white squares and EPP rosettes to make a total of sixteen EPP blocks.

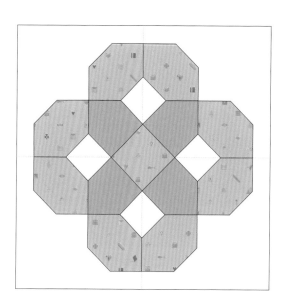

## QUILT LAYOUT

*Follow the layout diagram when constructing the quilt top.*

9   Arrange the EPP blocks into four rows of four blocks each, as shown. Each colourway is placed on a top-right-to-bottom-left diagonal, from left to right: light blue, mid blue, dark blue, turquoise, light turquoise, light green, mid green.

10  Using a ¼in seam allowance throughout, sew the blocks into rows and then sew the rows together.

## QUILTING AND FINISHING

11  Make a quilt sandwich of the quilt top, the wadding and the backing fabric. See **Quilt Techniques, Making a quilt sandwich**.

12  Quilt as desired. Mine was quilted with an all-over wave pattern. See **Quilt Techniques, Quilting**.

13  Square-up and bind to finish. See **Quilt Techniques, Squaring-up** and **Quilt Techniques, Binding**.

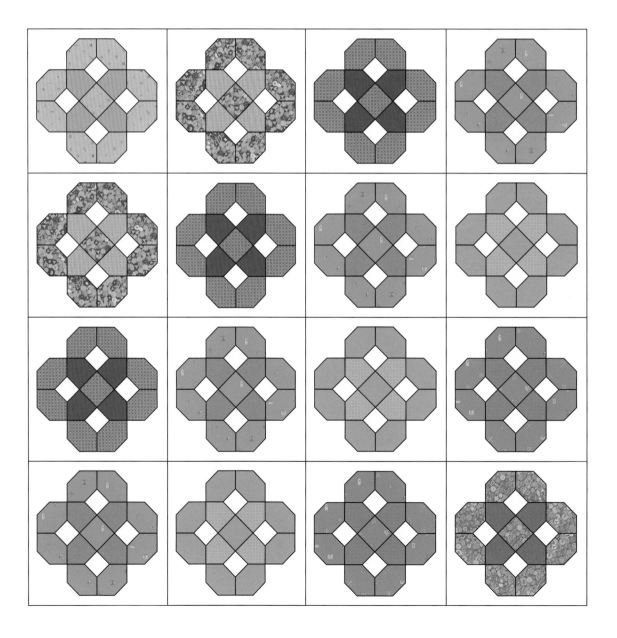

## TIP

*When constructing the quilt top, so the seam intersections nestle neatly, press the seams of each row in the same direction and the seams of alternate rows in the opposite direction. Press the long (horizontal) seams joining the rows to one side in the same direction each time (I pressed mine downwards).*

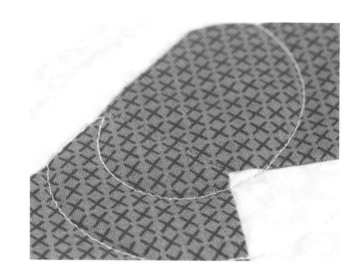

## COLOURING LAYOUT

# KALEIDOSCOPE KISSES

Large shapes combined with bold bright prints make this eye-popping quilt sing! Get creative with the colouring layout and see what secondary patterns you can come up with.

**Approximate size: 72 x 40in (183 x 102cm)**

## FABRIC REQUIREMENTS

- ½yd (50cm) each of four different whites/creams low-volume prints and/or solids
- ⅜yd (40cm) blue floral print
- ⅝yd (60cm) pink floral print
- ⅝yd (60cm) purple floral print
- One fat quarter each of three different blue solids/tone-on-tones
- ⅜yd (40cm) each of three different pink solids/tone-on-tones
- ⅜yd (40cm) each of three different purple solids/tone-on-tones
- 80 x 48in (203 x 122cm) of backing fabric
- ½yd (50cm) of binding fabric
- 80 x 48in (203 x 122cm) of wadding

## TEMPLATES

- Ninety-two Template A
- Eighty-eight Template B
- Eighty-eight Template C
- Eighty-eight Template D
- Ninety-two Template E

## TIPS

*For details about cutting and preparing shapes for EPP, see **How to EPP, Cutting and basting**.*

*If you like a narrower and tighter binding, cut your binding strips 2¼in wide (instead of 2½in wide).*

## CUTTING

*Before you start cutting out, decide where you are going to place each blue, pink and purple solid or tone-on-tone to ensure you cut out the correct EPP shapes. You may find the colouring layout useful for keeping track of your layout.*

### Whites/creams
· Twenty-three Template A from each fabric

### Blue floral print
· Sixteen Template B

### Pink floral print
· Thirty-two Template B

### Purple floral print
· Forty Template B

### Blue solids/tone-on-tones
· From one fat quarter: Sixteen Template C
· From one fat quarter: Sixteen Template D
· From one fat quarter: Twenty-four Template E

### Pink solids/tone-on-tones
· From one fabric: Thirty-two Template C
· From one fabric: Thirty-two Template D
· From one fabric: Thirty Template E

### Purple solids/tone-on-tones
· From one fabric: Forty Template C
· From one fabric: Forty Template D
· From one fabric: Thirty-eight Template E

### Binding fabric
· Six 2½in wide strips across the width of the fabric

## LOW-VOLUME KISSES BLOCKS

1    Take one Template A of each white/cream (four in total). Arrange as shown and sew together.

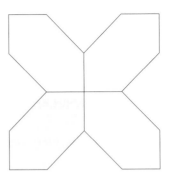

2    Repeat Step 1 to make a total of twenty-three low-volume units.

3    Take one low-volume unit and one pink Template E. Sew together as shown. This is a pink kisses side block. Repeat to make a total of six pink kisses side blocks.

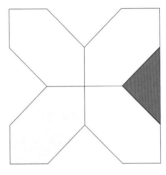

4    Take two low-volume units and two purple Template E. Repeat Step 3 to make a total of two purple kisses side blocks.

5    Take one low-volume unit and two blue Template E. Sew together as shown. This is a kisses corner block. Repeat to make a total of four kisses corner blocks.

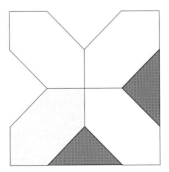

## KALEIDOSCOPE FULL BLOCKS

**6** Take four blue Template B, four blue Template C, four blue Template D and four blue Template E. Arrange as shown and sew together.

**7** Repeat Step 6 to make a total of four blue kaleidoscope full blocks.

**8** Working in the same manner as described in Step 6, make a total of six purple kaleidoscope full blocks.

## KALEIDOSCOPE EDGE BLOCKS

**9** Take four pink Template B, four pink Template C, four pink Template D and three pink Template E. Arrange as shown and sew together.

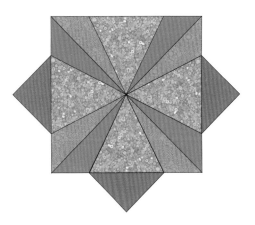

**10** Repeat Step 9 to make a total of eight pink kaleidoscope edge blocks.

**11** Working in the same manner as described in Step 9, make a total of four purple kaleidoscope edge blocks.

## TIP

*For details about sewing shapes and blocks together, see* **How to EPP, Sewing shapes and blocks together**.

## QUILT LAYOUT

*Follow the layout diagram when constructing the quilt top.*

**12** Arrange the kaleidoscope full blocks, kaleidoscope edge blocks, low-volume units, kisses side blocks and kisses corner blocks as shown, taking care to place and orientate the blocks and units as indicated.

**13** Sew the blocks and units together. To make the quilt top easier to handle, you can sew the blocks and units into rows and then sew the rows together.

**14** Once the quilt top is complete, remove all remaining paper pieces and then press.

## QUILTING AND FINISHING

**15** Make a quilt sandwich of the quilt top, the wadding and the backing fabric. See **Quilt Techniques, Making a quilt sandwich**.

**16** Quilt as desired. Mine was quilted with an all-over jagged straight-line pattern. See **Quilt Techniques, Quilting**.

**17** Square-up and bind to finish. See **Quilt Techniques, Squaring-up** and **Quilt Techniques, Binding**.

## COLOURING LAYOUT

# FLOWER POWER

This fun and simple hoop design is a great way to use up larger scraps from your stash. And as it's super-quick to make, it's an ideal last-minute gift too!

Approximate size: 15in (38cm) diameter

## FABRIC REQUIREMENTS

· One 5in (13cm) square of a multi-colour print
· One fat eighth of dark purple
· One fat eighth of light purple
· One fat eighth of mid-purple, solid or tone-on-tone
· One fat quarter of low-volume white or cream
· One fat quarter of light-coloured felt
· One fat quarter of wadding
· One 15in (38cm) diameter embroidery hoop
· Embroidery floss
· Ribbon or cord to hang, optional

## TEMPLATES

· One Template A
· Eight Template B
· Sixteen Template C

## TIPS

*If you have some larger pieces in your scrap bag, you may be able to cut the pieces for the EPP rosette (Templates A–C) from those.*

*For details about cutting and preparing shapes for EPP, see* **How to EPP, Cutting and basting**.

## CUTTING

### Multi-colour print
· One Template A

### Dark purple
· Eight Template B

### Light purple
· Eight Template C

### Mid-purple
· Eight Template C

### Felt
· Use the inside edge of inner ring of the embroidery hoop to draw a circle onto the felt and then cut out the circle just inside the drawn line

## EPP ROSETTE

1   Take Template A and the eight Template B. Arrange as shown and sew together to make the rosette centre.

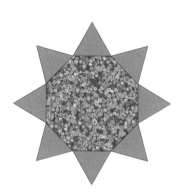

## TIPS

*For details about sewing shapes and blocks together, see* **How to EPP, Sewing shapes and blocks together**.

*For details about appliquéing EPP units to a background fabric, see* **How to EPP, Appliquéing EPP units in place**.

2   Take the eight light purple Template C and sew around the rosette centre as shown.

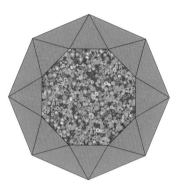

3   Take the eight mid-purple Template C and sew around the rosette centre made in Step 2 as shown. This completes the EPP rosette.

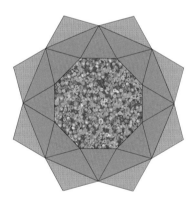

4   Press, remove all remaining paper pieces and then press again, making sure the outer seam allowance is neatly pressed under.

## APPLIQUÉING THE EPP ROSETTE

**5** Take the low-volume white or cream fat quarter. Lightly fold it in half lengthways and finger press. Open out and then lightly fold it in half widthways and finger press. Open out. This is your background fabric.

**6** Place the low-volume white or cream background fabric on a clean, flat surface with the right side facing upwards. Using the creased guidelines made in Step 5, right side up, position the EPP rosette centrally on top. Pin to secure.

**7** Appliqué the EPP rosette in place, tucking under any 'dog-ears' as you go. Press.

## QUILTING AND FINISHING

**8** Baste the EPP rosette/background fabric unit to the wadding. Place in the embroidery hoop, taking care to centre the EPP rosette. Pull evenly and firmly, making sure the fabric is smooth and tight in the hoop. Once the fabric is taut, tighten the screw to close the hoop.

**9** Using the embroidery floss, hand quilt as desired. On the background fabric, I stitched three rows of running stitch echoing the outer shape of the EPP rosette. I also stitched a line of running stitch around the outer edge of the light purple Template C shapes.

**10** Place the quilted unit/embroidery hoop right side down on a clean, flat surface. Using strong (e.g. quilting) thread, sew a large running stitch all around the outer edge of the hoop, approximately ½in beyond the hoop (you will be stitching through background fabric and wadding). Leave a long thread tail at the start and finish of your stitching on the wadding side.

**11** Place the thread tails inside the hoop. Then, cutting approximately ½in outside the line of running stitch made in Step 10, cut away the excess backing fabric and wadding.

**12** Pull the thread tails to gather up the remaining excess background fabric/wadding you now have on the wrong side of your hoop. Once it's gathered up tight, knot the thread tails to secure.

**13** To give a neat finish, place the felt circle on top of the gathered background fabric/wadding on the wrong side of your hoop. Whipstitch all the way around to secure the felt in place.

**14** Hang and enjoy!

## COLOURING LAYOUT

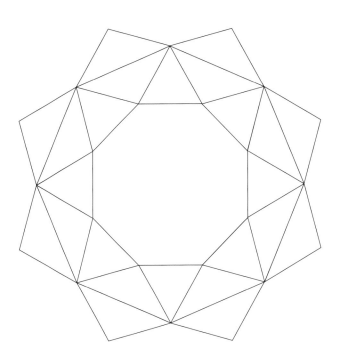

## TIP

*If you prefer, you can quilt by machine, but you will need to do this before you put the background fabric/wadding unit into the embroidery hoop.*

# OCEAN CIRCLE

Cosy up and drift away with this circular ocean-themed cushion – a super-comfortable addition to any sofa or armchair! Why not make one for each colour of the rainbow?

**Approximate size: 19in (48cm) diameter**

## FABRIC REQUIREMENTS

- One fat eighth each of three different blue/green/aqua solids or tone-on-tone
- One fat eighth each of five different blue/green/aqua prints
- One 21in (53.5cm) square for the cushion back
- 25in (63.5cm) square of wadding
- Filling/stuffing of your choice

## TEMPLATES

- Twenty Template A
- Fifty-five Template B
- Ten Template C

## TIP

*For details about cutting and preparing shapes for EPP, see **How to EPP, Cutting and basting**.*

## CUTTING

*Before you start cutting out, decide where you are going to place each fabric to ensure you cut out the correct EPP shapes. You may find the colouring layout useful for this.*

### Solids/tone-on-tones

· From one fat eighth: Eight Template A and three Template B
· From one fat eighth: Six Template A and four Template B
· From one fat eighth: Six Template A and three Template B

### Prints

· From one fat eighth: Nine Template B and four Template C
· From each of two fat eighths: Nine Template B and two Template C
· From each of two fat eighths: Nine Template B and one Template C

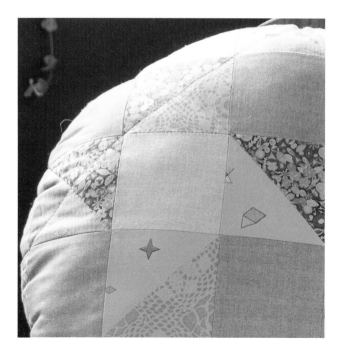

## TRIANGLE UNITS

**1** Take two different print Template B and sew them together on their long diagonal edge. This is a half-square triangle (HST).

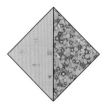

**2** Repeat Step 1 to make a total of twenty HSTs. (You will have five print Template B left over.)

**3** Take two different print Template C and sew them together on a short straight edge to create a triangle. This is a pieced edge triangle.

**4** Repeat Step 3 to make a total of five pieced edge triangles.

## TIP

*For details about sewing shapes and blocks together, see* **How to EPP, Sewing shapes and blocks together**.

# CUSHION FRONT

*When constructing the cushion front, refer to the layout diagram, making sure you orientate the HSTs as shown. You can follow my colour placements or create your own arrangement.*

**5**  Take five solid/tone-on-tone Template A, five solid/tone-on-tone Template B, one print Template B, four HSTs and one pieced edge triangle. Arrange as shown and sew together.

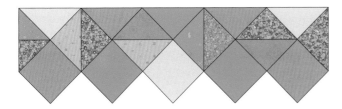

**6**  Take five solid/tone-on-tone Template A, one print Template B, four HSTs and one pieced edge triangle. Arrange as shown and sew together. Sew to the bottom of the unit made in Step 5.

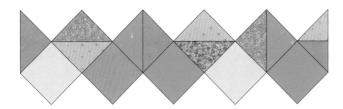

**7**  Take five solid/tone-on-tone Template A, one print Template B, four HSTs and one pieced edge triangle. Arrange as shown and sew together. Sew to the bottom of the unit made in Step 6.

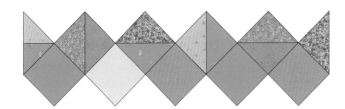

**8**  Take five solid/tone-on-tone Template A, one print Template B, four HSTs and one pieced edge triangle. Arrange as shown and sew together. Sew to the bottom of the unit made in Step 7.

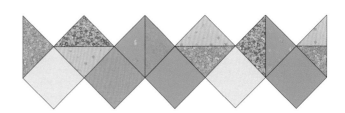

**9**  Take five solid/tone-on-tone Template B, one print Template B, four HSTs and one pieced edge triangle. Arrange as shown and sew together. Sew to the bottom of the unit made in Step 8.

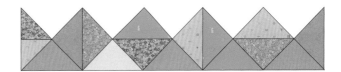

**10**  The cushion top is now complete. Press, remove all remaining paper pieces and then press again.

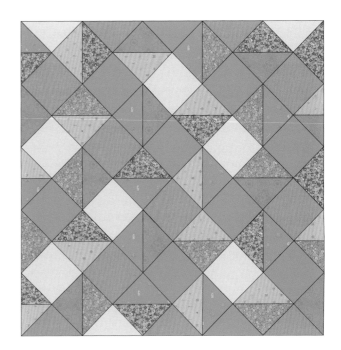

**11** Wrong sides together, fold the cushion top into quarters. To create a curve, starting from the centre point of the cushion top, measure and mark 10in along the folded edge. Then, keeping the 0 mark on the ruler on the centre point of the folded cushion top, move the ruler in 1in increments, marking 10in from the centre each time, until you get to the other edge (where two folded edges meet).

**12** Join up the marks to form a drawn quarter-circle curve.

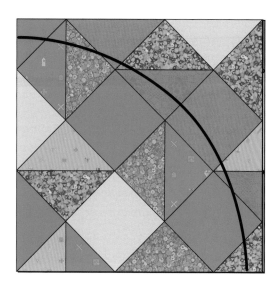

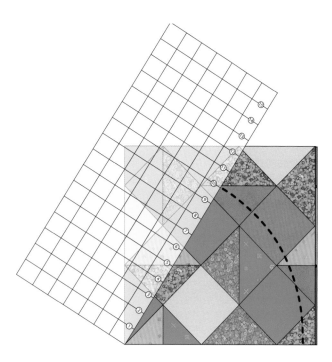

**13** Pin the fabric together, inside and outside the drawn line, to stop the fabric moving. Cut carefully along the drawn line, open out and press. This completes your cushion front.

**14** Take the 21in square and, using the cushion front as a template, cut out the cushion back.

## QUILTING AND FINISHING

**15** Baste the cushion front to the wadding.

**16** Quilt as desired. Mine was quilted in a simple grid pattern. See **Quilt Techniques, Quilting**.

**17** Trim away the excess wadding.

**18** Place the quilted cushion front and the cushion back right sides together. Pin in place. Sew all the way around using a ½in seam allowance, leaving an approximately 4in gap for turning.

## TIP

*If you'd rather not mark onto your fabric using a ruler, you could make a 10in-radius quarter-circle pattern piece from greaseproof or tracing paper. Pin this in place onto your folded cushion top and then cut around the outer edge of the pattern piece. Cut out your cushion back in the same manner.*

**19** Taking care not to snip into the stitching, clip out small triangles from the seam allowance at intervals of approximately 1in as shown, but do not clip in the turning gap. This will give the cushion a smoother finish when you turn it through.

**20** Turn the cushion right side out through the gap in the seam. Fill with your choice of filling/stuffing.

**21** Make sure the seam allowance is neatly tucked under inside the gap and then hand-sew the gap closed using a small ladder stitch.

## TIPS

*In Step 18, take a few backstitches at the start and end of your stitching.*

*Use lots of pins to keep the curve neatly together and sew slowly around the circle.*

## COLOURING LAYOUT

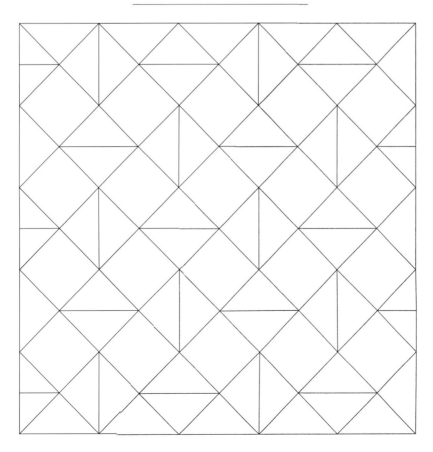

# COLOURFUL CROSSES

This EPP and appliquéd cushion will add a bold and stylish accent to any home décor scheme. And the graphic design is the perfect showcase for colourful prints and solids!

**Approximate size: 21in (53.5cm) square**

## FABRIC REQUIREMENTS

· One fat eighth each of five different prints
· One fat eighth each of four solids/tone-on-tones to match four of the prints
· One fat quarter of a solid/tone-on-tone to match the fifth print, includes binding
· 1¼yd (1.1m) of solid/linen texture for cushion front background and cushion back
· 25in (63.5cm) square of wadding
· 22in (56cm) square cushion pad

## TEMPLATES

· Thirty-six Template A
· Thirty-six Template B

## TIPS

*Instead of five different prints, I used a colour-gradient print with bands of different colours running along the lengthwise grain of the fabric. You may wish to use a similar type of fabric – you need bands approximately 2¾in (7cm) high. Or you could use prints from the same range in different colourways.*

*If you would like to use a different (sixth) colour for the binding, you will need one fat eighth each of five solids/tone-on-tones to match your five prints for the EPP blocks plus ¼yd (30cm) of binding fabric. (Cut three 2½in wide strips across the width of the fabric for the binding – or 2¼in wide strips if you prefer a narrower binding.) Alternatively, you could make a self-coloured binding with the leftover solid/linen texture.*

*For details about cutting and preparing shapes for EPP, see* **How to EPP, Cutting and basting**.

## CUTTING

### Prints

· From one fat eighth: Four Template A
· From each of four fat eighths: Eight Template A

### Fat eighth solids/tone-on-tones

*Cut the following pieces from each colour.*

· Eight Template B

### Fat quarter solid/tone-on-tone

· Four Template B
· Five 2½in wide strips across the width of the fat quarter for binding

### Solid/linen texture

· One 21½in square
· One 21½ x 17in rectangle
· One 21½ x 12in rectangle

## CUSHION FRONT

1   Take four Template A of the same colour. Arrange as shown and sew together.

## TIPS

*For details about sewing shapes and blocks together, see* **How to EPP, Sewing shapes and blocks together**.

*For details about appliquéing EPP units to a background fabric, see* **How to EPP, Appliquéing EPP units in place**.

2   Take four Template B of the same colourway and sew them to the unit made in Step 1 as shown. This completes one EPP block.

3   Repeat Steps 1 and 2 to make a total of nine EPP blocks. You will have two each of four colours and one of a fifth colour.

4   Arrange your blocks into three rows of three as shown. Sew the blocks into rows and then sew the rows together.

5   Press, remove all the paper pieces and then press again, making sure the outer seam allowance is neatly pressed under. This is your EPP unit.

6   Take the 21½in solid/linen texture square. This is your cushion front background. Place it on a clean, flat surface with the right side facing upwards. Position the EPP unit centrally on top. Pin to secure.

**7** Appliqué the EPP unit in place around its outer edges and also around the inner square-on-point 'gaps', tucking under any 'dog-ears' as you go. Press. This completes your cushion front.

## QUILTING AND FINISHING

**8** Baste the cushion front to the wadding.

**9** Quilt as desired. Mine was quilted on the background fabric, echoing the outer edge of the EPP unit and the square-on-point 'gaps'. See **Quilt Techniques, Quilting**.

**10** Square-up, trimming away the excess wadding.

**11** Take the solid/linen texture rectangles. On one long edge of each rectangle, turn over a ¼in hem and then turn over another ¼in. Press and then topstitch approximately ⅛in in from each folded edge using a longer stitch length than usual.

**12** Place the quilted cushion front on a clean, flat surface with the wrong side facing upwards. Wrong side down and matching up the raw edges along the bottom and sides of the cushion front, place the smaller rectangle on top – the neatened edge will run across the cushion front. In the same way, place the larger rectangle on top, matching up the raw edges along the top and sides of the cushion front. The cushion back pieces will overlap.

**13** Pin all around to secure. Using a longer stitch length than usual and stitching within the ¼in seam allowance, stay stitch all the way around the cushion. This will keep all the pieces in place for the next step.

**14** Bind as you would a quilt. See **Quilt Techniques, Binding**. Insert your cushion pad through the overlapped edges, plump up and enjoy!

## COLOURING LAYOUT

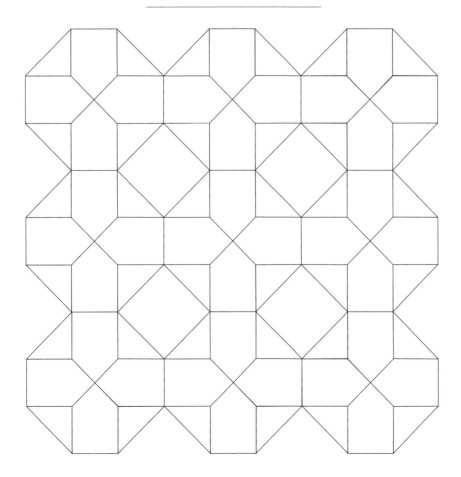

# IT'S ALL ABOUT THE HEXIES

Traditional hexies have been given a fun makeover in these bright potholders, bringing a modern twist to a household staple! It's also a great make for using up scraps.

**Approximate size of each potholder: 8½in (22cm) square**

*The fabric and template requirements are to make two potholders.*

## FABRIC REQUIREMENTS

· One fat eighth each of six different colours
· Two 2 x 5in (10 x 13cm) rectangles for hanging loops
· Two 9in (23cm) squares of backing fabric
· Four 9in (23cm) squares of heat-resistant wadding

## TEMPLATES

· Seventy-eight Template A

## TIP

*For details about cutting and preparing shapes for EPP, see **How to EPP, Cutting and basting**.*

## CUTTING

### Fat eighths

· Seventy-eight Template A in total – you could cut thirteen from each fabric, or more from some fabrics and fewer from others

## POTHOLDER FRONTS

*For each row of hexies use a good assortment of colours.*

**1** Take thirteen Template A, arrange as shown and sew together.

**2** Take another thirteen Template A and sew them to the bottom of the unit made in Step 1.

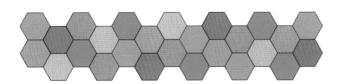

**3** Referring to the layout diagram, repeat Step 2 another four times to complete the potholder front made-fabric.

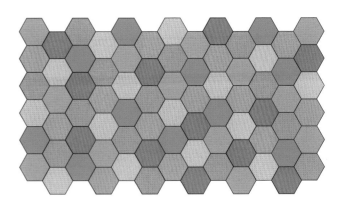

**4** Press and remove all remaining paper pieces, then press again.

**5** From the potholder front made-fabric cut two 9in squares.

**6** Using a longer stitch length than usual and stitching within the ¼in seam allowance, stay stitch all the way around the edge of each square to secure the hand-sewn seams.

## HANGING LOOPS

**7** Take one 2 x 5in rectangle. Wrong sides together, fold the strip in half lengthwise and press. Open out and then, wrong sides together, fold each long edge to the centre crease and press. Fold in half lengthwise so the folded edges meet up (the long raw edges are now enclosed) and press.

**8** Using a longer stitch length than usual, topstitch approximately ⅛in in from the edge where the folded edges meet up. This stitching will stop the folds from opening.

**9** Repeat Steps 7 and 8 with your remaining 2 x 5in rectangle. Put to one side.

## TIP

*For details about sewing shapes and blocks together, see* **How to EPP, Sewing shapes and blocks together**.

## FINISHING

**10** Take one 9in square potholder front and one 9in square of heat-resistant wadding. Matching up the raw edges, place the shiny side of wadding against the wrong side of the potholder front and baste in place to secure.

**11** Take one 9in square potholder backing and one 9in square of heat-resistant wadding. Matching up the raw edges, place the shiny side of wadding against the wrong side of the backing and baste in place.

**12** With the backing fabric facing upwards, place the backing/wadding unit on a clean, flat surface. Take one hanging loop strip and fold it in half so the short edges match up. Matching up the raw edges of the loop with the raw edges of the potholder, position it 1in in from either the top left-hand or top-right hand corner. If you wish, baste the loop in place.

**13** Matching up the raw edges, right sides together, place the potholder front/wadding unit on top. Pin or clip in place.

**14** Sew all the way around using a ¼in seam allowance, leaving a 3–4in gap for turning on one non-loop edge.

**15** Clip the corners to reduce bulk, taking care not to snip into the stitching.

**16** Turn right side out through the gap. Carefully poke the corners out and then lightly press to give crisp edges, making sure the seam allowance is neatly tucked under inside the gap.

**17** Topstitch all the way around the potholder, approximately ⅛in in from the edge, with a longer stitch length than usual. This will close the turning gap.

**18** Repeat Steps 10–17 to make the second potholder.

## COLOURING LAYOUT

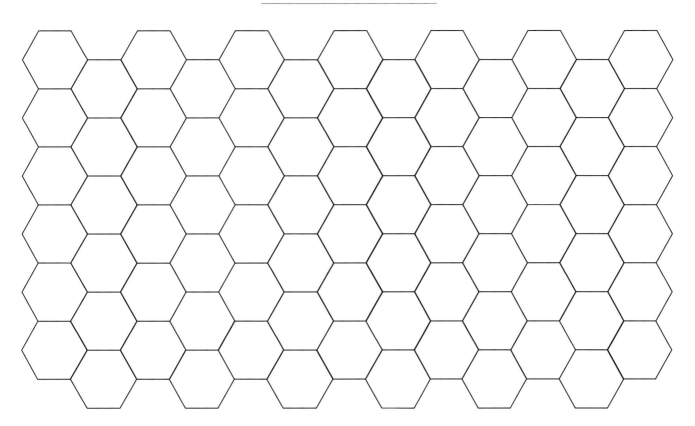

# COLOUR POP

This cheerful set of placemats and coasters will add a vibrant pop of colour to any table! Use up leftover fabrics to create a scrappy-style collection.

**Approximate size of each placemat: 11¾ x 14¾in (30 x 37.5cm)**

**Approximate size of each coaster: 6in (15cm) square**

*The fabric and template requirements are to make four placemats and four coasters.*

## FABRIC REQUIREMENTS

- ½yd (50cm) of bold multi-colour print
- One fat eighth each of two different solid/tone-on-tone blues
- One fat eighth each of two different solid/tone-on-tone greens
- One fat eighth each of two different solid/tone-on-tone pinks
- One fat eighth each of two different solid/tone-on-tone purples
- One fat eighth each of two different solid/tone-on-tone yellows
- ⅝yd (60cm) of grey
- Four 14 x 17in (35.5 x 43cm) rectangles of backing fabric for placemats
- ½yd (50cm) of binding fabric for placemats
- Four 14 x 17in (35.5 x 43cm) rectangles of wadding for placemats
- One fat quarter of backing fabric for coasters
- Four 8in (20cm) squares of wadding for coasters

## TEMPLATES

- Forty-eight Template A
- Ninety-six Template B
- Fifty-two Template C
- Thirty-two Template D
- Thirty-two Template E
- Forty Template F

## TIP

*Try using different tones of the same colour for a sophisticated look, or ring the changes with seasonal prints.*

# PLACEMATS

*The following instructions are for making one placemat.*

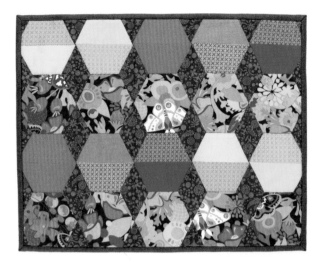

## Cutting

### BOLD MULTI-COLOUR

· Ten Template A

### BLUES, GREENS, PINKS, PURPLES, YELLOWS

· Two Template B from each solid/tone-on-tone

### GREY

· Twelve Template C

· Four Template D

· Six Template E

· Eight Template F

### BINDING FABRIC

· Six 2¼in wide strips across the width of the fabric

# TIP

*For details about cutting and preparing shapes for EPP, see* **How to EPP, Cutting and basting**.

## Placemat assembly

1   Take one Template B of each blues and sew them together as shown to make one split hexagon. Repeat with the remaining blues Template B.

2   Repeat Step 1 for the greens, pinks, purples and yellows Template B. You will have two split hexagons of each colourway – ten in total.

3   Take five bold multi-colour Template A, two grey Template D and four grey Template F. Arrange as shown and sew together.

4   Take four grey Template C and two grey Template E and sew them to the bottom of the row made in Step 3 as shown.

5   Take one split hexagon of each colourway and sew them to the bottom of the row made in Step 4 as shown.

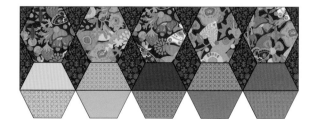

**6** Take four grey Template C and two grey Template E and sew them to the bottom of the row made in Step 5 as shown.

**9** Take one split hexagon of each colourway, two grey Template D and four grey Template F and sew them to the bottom of the row made in Step 8 as shown. This completes the placemat top.

**7** Take five bold multi-colour Template A and sew them to the bottom of the row made in Step 6.

**10** Press and then remove all remaining paper pieces.

## Quilting and finishing

**11** Make a quilt sandwich of the placemat top, a 14 x 17in rectangle of wadding and a 14 x 17in rectangle of backing fabric. See **Quilt Techniques, Making a quilt sandwich**.

**12** Quilt as desired. Mine was quilted using a simple straight-line vertical and horizontal grid. See **Quilt Techniques, Quilting**.

**13** Square-up and bind to finish. See **Quilt Techniques, Squaring-up** and **Quilt Techniques, Binding**.

**14** Repeat Steps 1–13 to make another three placemats. You will have enough binding to bind all four placemats.

**8** Take four grey Template C and two grey Template E and sew them to the bottom of the row made in Step 7 as shown.

## TIP

*For details about sewing shapes together, see* **How to EPP, Sewing shapes and blocks together**.

# COASTERS

*The following instructions are for making one coaster.*

## Cutting

### BOLD MULTI-COLOUR

· Two Template A

### BLUES, GREENS, PINKS, PURPLES, YELLOWS

· A total of four Template B (two pairs of two different colourways in the colours of your choice)

### GREY

· One Template C

· Four Template D

· Two Template E

· Two Template F

### BACKING FABRIC

· One 6in (15cm) square

# TIP

*For details about cutting and preparing shapes for EPP, see* **How to EPP, Cutting and basting**.

## Coaster assembly

**15**  Take one pair of Template B and sew them together to make one split hexagon. Repeat for the remaining pair. (See Step 1.)

**16**  Take one bold multi-colour Template A, one split hexagon, two grey Template D and one grey Template F. Arrange as shown and sew together.

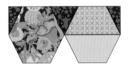

**17**  Take one grey Template C and two grey Template E and sew them to the bottom of the row made in Step 16 as shown.

**18**  Take one bold multi-colour Template A, one split hexagon, two grey Template D and one grey Template F and sew them to the bottom of the row made in Step 17 as shown. This completes the coaster top.

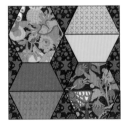

**19**  Press and then remove all remaining paper pieces.

## Quilting and finishing

**20** Baste the coaster onto an 8in square of wadding and then quilt as desired. Mine was quilted using a simple straight-line vertical and horizontal grid. See **Quilt Techniques, Quilting**.

**21** Keeping the design centred, trim the quilted coaster to 6in square. Place the coaster and a 6in square of backing fabric right sides together. Pin to secure.

**22** Sew all the way around using a ¼in seam allowance, leaving an approximately 1½in gap for turning on one edge. To secure the seam, take a few backstitches at the start and end of your stitching.

**23** Clip the corners to reduce bulk, taking care not to snip into the stitching.

**24** Turn right side out through the gap. Press, making sure the seam allowance is neatly tucked under inside the gap.

**25** Topstitch all the way around the coaster, approximately ⅛in in from the edge, with a longer stitch length than usual. This will close the turning gap.

**26** Repeat Steps 15–25 to make another three coasters.

## TIP

*For details about sewing shapes and blocks together, see* **How to EPP, Sewing shapes and blocks together**.

## COLOURING LAYOUTS

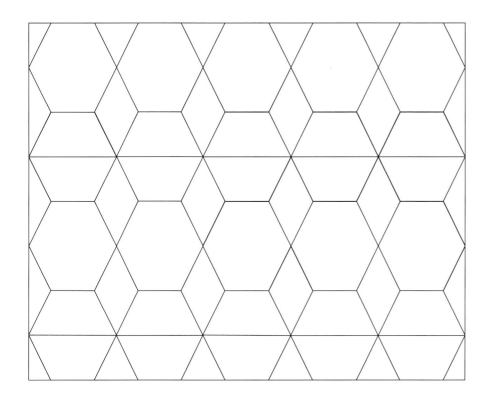

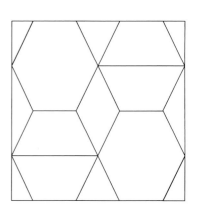

# DROPLETS BUCKET

This handy storage bucket is perfect for storing fabrics, notions and stationery. Why not make a few to brighten up your living spaces and work areas?

**Approximate size: 10½in (27cm) high x 9in (23cm) wide x 5in (13cm) deep**

## FABRIC REQUIREMENTS

- ½yd (50cm) of bold print
- One fat eighth of light solid or tone-on-tone
- ½yd (50cm) of medium solid or tone-on-tone
- Two 16 x 15in (40.5 x 38cm) rectangles for lining
- Two 13 x 14in (33 x 35.5cm) rectangle of foam stabiliser

## TEMPLATES

- Forty Template A
- Twenty-four Template B
- Twelve Template C
- Twenty-four Template D

## TIPS

*If you wish, for a coordinated look, for the lining fabric you could use the same light or medium solid or tone-on-tone fabric used in the EPP panel.*

*For details about cutting and preparing shapes for EPP, see* **How to EPP, Cutting and basting***.*

## CUTTING

### Bold print
· Forty Template A

### Light solid/tone-on-tone
· Twenty-four Template B

### Medium solid/tone-on-tone
· Twelve Template C
· Twenty-four Template D

## EPP PANELS

1   Take five Template A and six Template D. Arrange as shown and sew together.

2   Take five Template A and six Template B and sew them to the bottom of the unit made in Step 1.

3   Take six Template C and sew them to the bottom of the unit made in Step 2.

## TIP

*For details about sewing shapes and blocks together, see* **How to EPP, Sewing shapes and blocks together**.

**4** Take five Template A and six Template B and sew them to the bottom of the unit made in Step 3.

**5** Take five Template A and six Template D and sew them to the bottom of the unit made in Step 4. This completes one EPP panel.

**6** Repeat Steps 1–5 to make a second EPP panel.

**7** Once both panels are complete, press, remove all remaining paper pieces and then press again.

## BUCKET PANELS

**8** Trim each EPP panel to 14 x 15in.

**9** From each bottom corner of each EPP rectangle, cut away a 3in square.

**10** Take the two foam stabiliser rectangles and from each bottom corner of each rectangle cut away a 3in square.

**11** Take one EPP rectangle and place it on a clean, flat surface with the wrong side facing upwards. Take one foam stabiliser rectangle and centre it on top of the EPP rectangle – there should be ½in of the EPP rectangle showing all the way around. Baste the stabiliser in place.

**12** Quilt as desired. Mine has been quilted in vertical straight lines. See **Quilt Techniques, Quilting**. This completes one bucket panel.

**13** Repeat Steps 11 and 12 with the second EPP and foam stabiliser rectangles to make a second bucket panel.

# CONSTRUCTING THE BUCKET

**14** Place the bucket panels right sides together (i.e. EPP sides facing each other). Sew down both side edges and along the bottom edge using a ½in seam allowance. Do not sew around the 3in edges where you have cut away the 3in squares.

**15** Working on one bottom corner at a time, re-fold the bag so the end of the bottom seam meets the end of the side seam. The raw edges of the cut-away squares will now match up to form a boxed corner. Pin and then sew across the raw edges of the corner with a ½in seam allowance, taking a few backstitches at the start and end of your stitching to secure the seam.

**16** Repeat Step 15 to form the other boxed corner. This is the EPP bucket.

**17** Take the two lining rectangles and from each bottom corner of each rectangle cut away a 3in square.

**18** Repeat Steps 15 and 16 with the lining rectangles, but this time leave an approximate 3in turning gap along the bottom seam. This is the bucket lining.

**19** Turn the EPP bucket right side out. With the lining still wrong side out, place the EPP bucket inside the lining, i.e. right sides will be against each other. Match up the top raw edges, making sure the side seams are aligned. Pin or clip in place. Sew all the way around the top edge using a ½in seam allowance.

**20** Turn the bucket right side out through the gap in the bottom seam of the lining. Carefully poke out the corners of the bucket and then push the lining neatly down inside the bucket. The lining is higher than the EPP bucket (approximately 1in higher), so pull up the extra lining fabric all the way around the bucket. Once it is neatly arranged, press the lining at the top of the bucket.

**21** Fold the extra lining over onto the right side of the bucket, making sure the side seams are aligned. Press and then pin or clip in place.

**22** Using a longer stitch length than usual, topstitch the lining band in place close to its top and bottom edges.

**23** Make sure the seam allowance is neatly tucked under inside the gap and then hand-sew the gap in the bottom seam of the lining closed using a small ladder stitch. Your bucket is now ready to fill with goodies!

## COLOURING LAYOUT

# RAINBOW STARS

This striking quilt will look equally great on the wall or sofa. Even in the depths of winter, the bright colours will warm you up with thoughts of balmy summer evenings.

**Approximate size: 53 x 38in (135 x 96.5cm)**

## FABRIC REQUIREMENTS

- One fat quarter each of the following prints: orange, yellow, green, blue, purple, pink
- One fat eighth of a light orange solid/tone-on-tone
- One fat quarter each of the following light solids/tone-on-tones: yellow, green, blue, purple, pink
- One fat quarter of a dark orange solid/tone-on-tone
- One fat eighth each of the following dark solids/tone-on-tones: yellow, green, blue, purple, pink
- 61 x 46in (155 x 117cm) of backing fabric
- ⅜yd (40cm) of binding fabric
- 61 x 46in (155 x 117cm) of wadding

## TEMPLATES

- Eighty-eight Template A
- Seventy-three Template B
- Twenty Template C
- Eighty-four Template D
- Eighty-eight Template E
- Four Template F
- Eight Template G
- Thirty Template H

## TIPS

*For details about cutting and preparing shapes for EPP, see* **How to EPP, Cutting and basting**.

*If you like a narrower and tighter binding, cut your binding strips 2¼in wide (instead of 2½in wide).*

## CUTTING

### Orange print
· Eight Template A
· Four Template D
· Eight Template E
· Eight Template G

### Yellow, green, blue, purple, pink prints
*Cut the following pieces from each colour.*
· Sixteen Template A
· Sixteen Template D
· Sixteen Template E

### Light orange
· Four Template F

### Light yellow, green, blue, purple, pink
*Cut the following pieces from each colour.*
· Fourteen Template B
· Four Template H

### Dark orange
· Three Template B
· Ten Template H

### Dark yellow, green, blue, purple, pink
*Cut the following pieces from each colour.*
· Four Template C

### Binding fabric
· Five 2½in wide strips across the width of the fabric

◇ ◇ ◇ ◇ ◇ ◇ ◇ ◇ ◇ ◇ ◇ ◇ ◇ ◇

## TIPS

*Keep your templates grouped together for each colourway. For ease of identification, you could label the back of each template, e.g. 'A', 'B', etc. Then everything will be organised for when you start making the blocks.*

*For details about sewing shapes and blocks together, see* **How to EPP, Sewing shapes and blocks together***.*

## LARGE BLOCKS

**1** Take four yellow Template A. Arrange as shown and sew together to make the block centre.

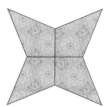

**2** Take four yellow Template B and sew them to the block centre made in Step 1 as shown. This completes one large block.

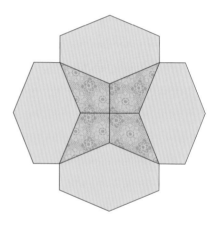

**3** Working as described in Steps 1 and 2, make the following large blocks:

· Three yellow
· Three green
· Three blue
· Three purple
· Three pink

You will have fifteen large blocks in total.

## LARGE EDGE BLOCKS

**4** Take two yellow Template A, one yellow Template B and two yellow Template H. Arrange as shown and sew together.

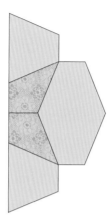

**5** Working as described in Step 4, make the following large edge blocks:

- Two yellow
- Two green
- Two blue
- Two purple
- Two pink
- Three orange

You will have thirteen large edge blocks in total.

## LARGE CORNER BLOCKS

**6** Take one orange Template A and two orange Template H. Arrange as shown and sew together.

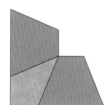

**7** Repeat Step 6 to make a total of two orange large corner blocks.

## STAR BLOCKS

**8** Take one yellow Template C, four yellow Template D and four yellow Template E. Arrange as shown and sew together.

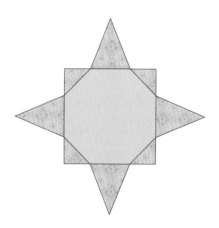

**9** Working as described in Step 8, make the following star blocks:

- Four yellow
- Four green
- Four blue
- Four purple
- Four pink

You will have twenty star blocks in total.

## STAR EDGE BLOCKS

**10** Take one orange Template D, two orange Template E, one orange Template F and two orange Template G. Arrange as shown and sew together.

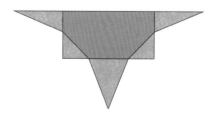

**11** Repeat Step 10 to make a total of four orange star edge blocks.

# QUILT LAYOUT

*Follow the layout diagram when constructing the quilt top.*

**12** Arrange the large blocks, large edge blocks, large corner blocks, star blocks and star edge blocks as shown.

**13** Sew the blocks together. To make the quilt top easier to handle, you can sew the blocks together into rows and then sew the rows together.

**14** Once the quilt top is complete, remove all remaining paper pieces and then press.

## QUILTING AND FINISHING

**15** Make a quilt sandwich of the quilt top, the wadding and the backing fabric. See **Quilt Techniques, Making a quilt sandwich**.

**16** Quilt as desired. Mine was quilted with an all-over jagged straight-line pattern. See **Quilt Techniques, Quilting**.

**17** Square-up and bind to finish. See **Quilt Techniques, Squaring-up** and **Quilt Techniques, Binding**.

## COLOURING LAYOUT

# TUMBLING WHEELS

This bright wall hanging with its geometric modern feel would look stunning in any room of the home. And the scrappy binding adds an extra pop of colour!

**Approximate size: 41 x 25in (104 x 63.5cm), excluding tabs**

## FABRIC REQUIREMENTS

· ¾yd (70cm) of white solid/tone-on-tone
· One fat quarter each of the following solids: green, orange, pink, yellow
· One fat eighth each of the following floral prints: green, orange, pink, yellow
· One fat eighth each of the following tone-on-tone prints: green, orange, pink, yellow
· One fat eighth each of the following prints: green, orange, pink, yellow
· 46 x 30in (117 x 76cm) of backing fabric
· 46 x 30in (117 x 76cm) of wadding

## TEMPLATES

· Thirty-nine Template A
· Thirty-nine Template B
· Thirty-nine Template C
· Thirty-nine Template D

## TIPS

*For details about cutting and preparing shapes for EPP, see **How to EPP, Cutting and basting**.*

*If you like a narrower and tighter binding, cut your binding strips (floral prints) 2¼in wide (instead of 2½in wide). If you prefer a single-fabric binding, you require ⅜yd (40cm), from which you need to cut four 2½in (or 2¼in) wide strips across the width of the fabric.*

# CUTTING

### White solid/tone-on-tone

· One 26 x 42in rectangle

### Green solid

· Twelve Template A

· One 4 x 6in rectangle

### Orange, pink, yellow solids

*Cut the following pieces from each colour.*

· Nine Template A

· One 4 x 6in rectangle

### Green floral print

· Twelve Template B

· Two 2½in wide strips across the width of the fat eighth for binding

### Orange, pink, yellow floral prints

*Cut the following pieces from each colour.*

· Nine Template B

· Two 2½in wide strips across the width of the fat eighth for binding

### Green tone-on-tone print

· Twelve Template C

### Orange, pink, yellow tone-on-tone prints

*Cut the following pieces from each colour.*

· Nine Template C

### Green print

· Twelve Template D

### Orange, pink, yellow prints

*Cut the following pieces from each colour.*

· Nine Template D

## TIP

*For details about sewing shapes and blocks together, see* **How to EPP, Sewing shapes and blocks together**.

# EPP PANEL

**1**  Take one green Template B, one green Template C and one green Template D. Arrange as shown and sew together. This completes one EPP pieced triangle.

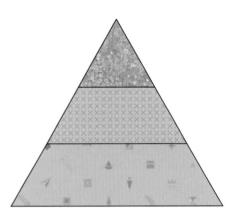

**2**  Repeat Step 1 to make a total of three green EPP pieced triangles.

**3**  Take the three green EPP pieced triangles and three green Template A. Arrange as shown and sew together. This completes one EPP block.

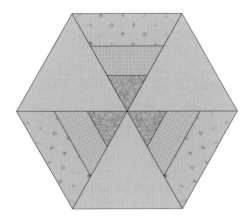

**4** Working as described in Steps 1–3, make the following EPP blocks:

- · Four green
- · Three orange
- · Three pink
- · Three yellow

You will have thirteen EPP blocks in total.

**5** Arrange the blocks as shown and sew together.

**6** Press, remove all remaining paper pieces and then press again, making sure the outer seam allowance is neatly pressed under.

## APPLIQUÉING THE EPP PANEL

**7** Take the white solid/tone-on-tone rectangle. Lightly fold it in half lengthways and finger press. Open out and then lightly fold it in half widthways and finger press. Open out. This is your background fabric.

**8** Place the background fabric right side up. Using the creased guidelines made in Step 7, right side up, position the EPP panel centrally on top. Pin to secure.

**9** Appliqué the EPP panel in place, tucking under any 'dog-ears' as you go. Press.

## HANGING TABS

**10** Take the green 4 x 6in rectangle. On each long edge, turn over a ¼in seam to the wrong side and press. Wrong sides together, fold the strip in half lengthwise, so the neatened long edges match up, and press. Topstitch approximately ⅛in in from each long edge using a longer stitch length than usual.

**11** Repeat Step 10 with your orange, pink and yellow 4 x 6in rectangles.

**12** Fold each strip in half so the raw edges match up. These will form your hanging tabs when attached to the wall hanging.

## QUILTING AND FINISHING

**13** Make a quilt sandwich of the wall hanging top, the wadding and the backing fabric. See **Quilt Techniques, Making a quilt sandwich**.

**14** Quilt as desired. Mine was quilted with a straight-line trellis pattern. See **Quilt Techniques, Quilting**.

**15** Square-up so the quilt measures approximately 41 x 25in. See **Quilt Techniques, Squaring-up**.

**16** Place the wall hanging on a clean, flat surface with the backing fabric facing upwards. Take the hanging tabs and place them evenly along the top edge of the hanging, matching up the raw edges of the tabs with the top raw edges of the hanging. Pin in place.

**17** Prepare your binding. See **Quilt Techniques, Binding**. Machine stitch the binding to the back of the hanging (not the front). This will trap the hanging tabs in the seam so they are securely attached. Fold the binding over to the front of the hanging and neatly hand-stitch in place.

## TIP

*For details about appliquéing EPP units to a background fabric, see* **How to EPP, Appliquéing EPP units in place**.

# COLOURING LAYOUT

# COMFY CUBE

This large cube pouffe features a beautiful EPP top and the plain sides are the perfect way to show off favourite fat quarters you can't bear to cut into!

Approximate size: 17½in (44.5cm) cube

## FABRIC REQUIREMENTS

- One fat eighth each of four different orange tones
- One fat eighth each of three different yellow tones
- One fat eighth each of two different mustard tones
- One fat eighth each of seven different green tones
- One fat quarter each of five different colours for the sides and base of the pouffe
- 22in (56cm) square of wadding
- Bean bag filling or toy stuffing

## TEMPLATES

- Fifty-five Template A
- Twenty-seven Template B
- Six Template C

## TIP

*Colour match your cube to your living space scheme. These pouffes are great for kids' bedrooms, too!*

## CUTTING

*Before you start cutting out, decide where you are going to place each fabric to ensure you cut out the correct EPP shapes. You may find the colouring layout useful for keeping track of your layout.*

### Oranges

· From one fat eighth: Six Template A
· From one fat eighth: Five Template A
· From one fat eighth: Five Template B
· From one fat eighth: Four Template B and two Template C

### Yellows

· From one fat eighth: Six Template A
· From one fat eighth: Five Template A
· From one fat eighth: Four Template B and two Template C

### Mustards

· From one fat eighth: Six Template A
· From one fat eighth: Five Template A

### Greens

· From each of two fat eighths: Six Template A
· From each of two fat eighths: Five Template A
· From each of two fat eighths: Five Template B
· From one fat eighth: Four Template B and two Template C

### Fat quarter colours

· From each fat quarter: One 18in square

## TIP

*For details about cutting and preparing shapes for EPP, see* **How to EPP, Cutting and basting**.

## TIP

*For details about sewing shapes and blocks together, see* **How to EPP, Sewing shapes and blocks together**.

## EPP PANEL

1   Take the oranges Template As, Template Bs and Template Cs. Arrange as shown and sew together.

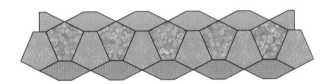

2   Take the yellows Template As, Template Bs and Template Cs and sew them to the bottom of the panel made in Step 1 as shown.

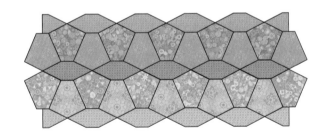

**3**  Take the mustards Templates As and sew them to the bottom of the panel made in Step 2 as shown.

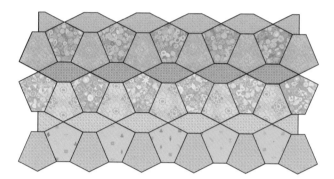

**4**  Take the greens Template As, Template Bs and Template Cs and sew them to the bottom of the panel made in Step 3 as shown.

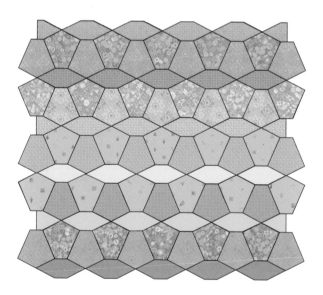

**5**  Press and then remove all remaining paper pieces.

**6**  Square-up the EPP panel as shown. It should measure 18in square.

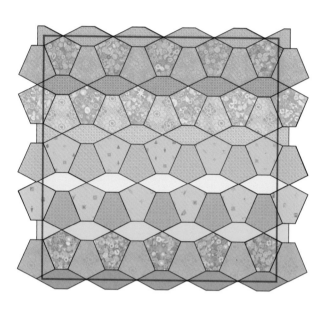

**7**  Baste the EPP panel onto the 22in square of wadding and quilt as desired. Mine was quilted using a simple straight-line vertical and horizontal grid using thread to blend in with the fabric colours. See **Quilt Techniques, Quilting**. Once quilted, trim away the excess wadding.

## TIP

*When squaring-up the EPP panel, draw an 18in square on top of the panel and then trim away the excess fabric.*

# CONSTRUCTING THE POUFFE

**8** Arrange the EPP panel and the five 18in fat quarter squares (Panels 1–5) as shown. Panel 3 will form the pouffe's base.

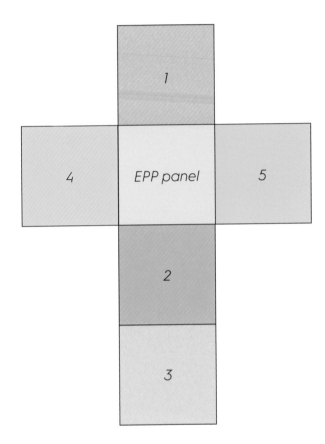

## TIPS

*When constructing the cube:*

· *Make sure you join the pieces on the correct edge as indicated in the instructions*

· *When sewing the seams, unless instructed otherwise, start and stop ¼in in from the end each time, taking a few backstitches at the start and end of your stitching to secure the seam*

· *After sewing each seam, open out the seam and press*

**9** Place Panel 1 and the EPP panel right sides together. Pin or clip to secure. Sew together along the top edge of the EPP panel.

**10** Place Panel 2 and the EPP panel right sides together. Pin or clip to secure. Sew together along the bottom edge of the EPP panel.

**11** Place Panel 3 and Panel 2 right sides together. Pin or clip to secure. Sew together along the bottom edge of Panel 2.

**12** Place Panel 4 and the EPP panel right sides together. Pin or clip to secure. Sew together along the left-hand edge of the EPP panel.

**13** Place Panel 5 and the EPP panel right sides together. Pin or clip to secure. Sew together along the right-hand edge of the EPP panel.

**14** Place Panel 1 and Panel 4 right sides together. Pin or clip to secure. Starting at the top corner (the corner closest to the EPP panel), sew together. This forms the first side seam.

**15** Place Panel 1 and Panel 5 right sides together. Pin or clip to secure. Starting at the top corner (the corner closest to the EPP panel), sew together. This forms the second side seam.

**16** Place Panel 2 and Panel 4 right sides together. Pin or clip to secure. Starting at the top corner (the corner closest to the EPP panel), sew together. This forms the third side seam.

**17** Place Panel 2 and Panel 5 right sides together. Pin or clip to secure. Starting at the top corner (the corner closest to the EPP panel), sew together. This forms the final side seam.

**18** To complete the cube, Panel 3 (the base) needs to be joined to Panels 1, 4 and 5. Keep the cube wrong side out. Place Panel 3 and Panel 4 right sides together. Pin or clip to secure, then sew together.

**19** Place Panel 3 and Panel 1 right sides together. Pin or clip to secure, then sew together.

**20** Place Panel 3 and Panel 5 right sides together. Pin or clip to secure. This time, start sewing from the end of the seam (do not start ¼in in). Sew for approximately 5in, leave a 4in gap for turning and then sew to the end of the seam (do not end ¼in in). Take a few backstitches whenever you start or stop sewing as this will secure the seam.

**21** Clip the corners to reduce bulk, taking care not to snip into the stitching.

**22** Turn the pouffe right side out through the gap in the seam between Panels 3 and 5. Poke out all the corners using a chopstick or a point tool. Fill with your choice of filling/stuffing.

**23** Make sure the seam allowance is neatly tucked under inside the gap and then hand-sew the gap closed using a small ladder stitch.

## COLOURING LAYOUT

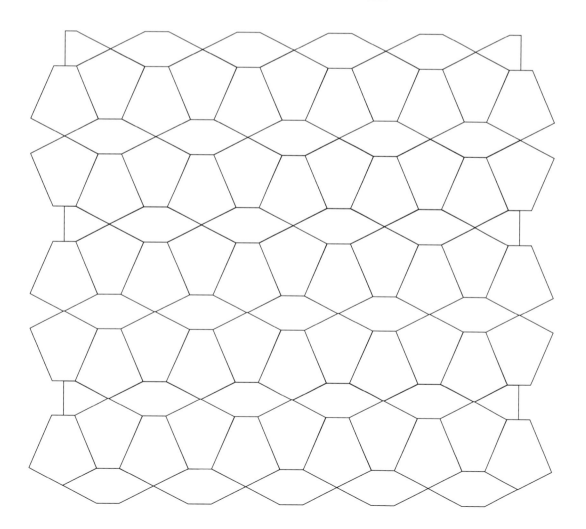

# STAR FOR A STAR

This starry mug rug is the perfect size for a large mug and a few cheeky biscuits on the side. An ideal little gift, it's also a fun way to use up scraps left over from previous projects!

**Approximate size: 7 x 11½in (18 x 28.5cm)**

## FABRIC REQUIREMENTS

· One 2½ x 4in (6.5 x 10cm) rectangle from each of four different star fabrics
· One 7in (18cm) star background square
· One 7 x 5in (18 x 13cm) background rectangle
· One 9 x 14in (23 x 35.5cm) rectangle of backing fabric
· One 9 x 14in (23 x 35.5cm) rectangle of wadding
· Two 2¼in (6cm) wide strips across the width of the fabric for binding
· Embroidery floss in colours to match the star fabrics

## TEMPLATES

· Four Template A

## TIPS

*You may be able to use binding strips left over from a previous project. If you wish, you could join shorter lengths of fabric to bring the binding strip up to approximately 42in (107cm) long – you could even join strips of different colours to give a multi-coloured binding.*

*For details about cutting and preparing shapes for EPP, see* **How to EPP, Cutting and basting**.

# CUTTING

## Star fabrics

· Four Template A

## EPP STAR BLOCK

1   Take the four Template A. Arrange as shown and sew together to make the star.

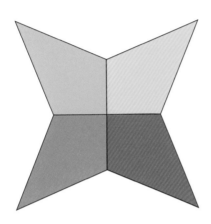

2   Press, remove the paper pieces and then press again, making sure the outer seam allowance is neatly pressed under.

3   Take the 7in star background square. Lightly fold it in half on one diagonal and finger press. Open out and then lightly fold it in half on the other diagonal and finger press. Open out.

4   Place the star background square right side up. Using the creased guidelines made in Step 3, right side up, position the EPP star centrally on top. Pin to secure.

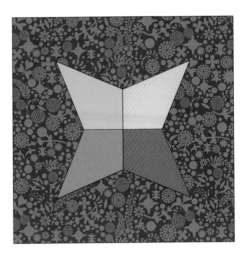

5   Appliqué the EPP star in place, tucking under any 'dog-ears' as you go. Press. This is your EPP star block.

## MUG RUG TOP

6   Matching up the raw edges on the left-hand edge of the star block, right sides together, place the 7 x 5in background rectangle on top of the EPP star block. Sew together with a ¼in seam allowance.

7   Open out and press, pressing the seam allowance towards the star background square.

## TIPS

*For details about sewing shapes and blocks together, see* **How to EPP, Sewing shapes and blocks together**.

*For details about appliquéing EPP units to a background fabric, see* **How to EPP, Appliquéing EPP units in place**.

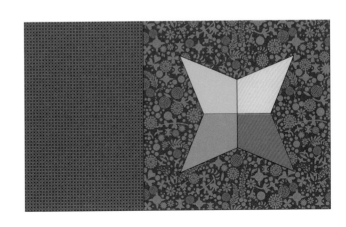

## QUILTING AND FINISHING

8    Baste the mug rug top to the wadding.

9    Hand quilt as desired. Using threads to match the star fabrics, I running stitched evenly-spaced horizontal lines on the background rectangle, and then used one of the threads to sew a row of running stitch around the EPP star, echoing its outer shape.

10   Baste the backing fabric to the quilted mug rug top to make a quilt sandwich. Trim away the excess backing and wadding.

11   Bind to finish. See **Quilt Techniques, Binding**.

## TIP

*If you prefer, you can quilt the mug rug by machine, but you will need to make a quilt sandwich of the mug rug top, the wadding and the backing fabric before quilting. See* **Quilt Techniques, Making a quilt sandwich** *and* **Quilt Techniques, Quilting**. *Then square up and bind to finish. See* **Quilt Techniques, Squaring-up** *and* **Quilt Techniques, Binding**.

## COLOURING LAYOUT

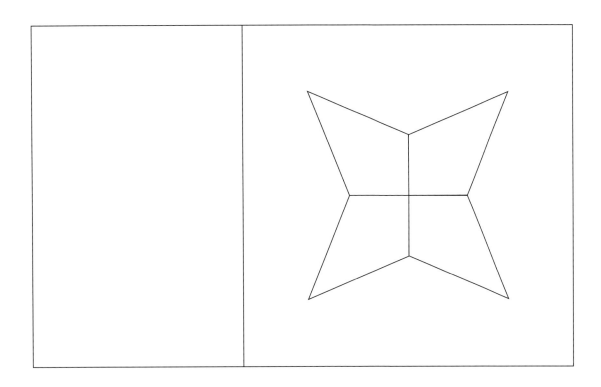

# QUILT TECHNIQUES

## MAKING A QUILT SANDWICH

Prior to quilting, the quilt top (or other pieced top, such as a cushion front), wadding and backing fabric are basted together to make a quilt sandwich. The backing fabric and wadding are cut 2–4in bigger all around than the top.

1   Place the backing fabric on a clean, flat surface with the wrong side facing upwards. Smooth it out to make sure there are no wrinkles. Spread out the wadding on top and then place the quilt top, right side up, centrally on top.

2   To baste the layers together, you can either use curved safety pins or quilt basting spray. If you are pinning your quilt sandwich, I suggest starting in the middle of the quilt and working your way outwards. If you are using quilt basting spray, I suggest you use the roll-and-spray method. Place the wadding on a clean, flat surface, centre the quilt top on top and then roll the bottom edge of the quilt top up to meet the top. Spray onto the wadding and roll a small section of the quilt top down onto the sprayed area. Smooth out from the centre, and repeat until the entire quilt top is basted. Repeat for the backing.

## QUILTING

If you wish, you can quilt by machine. For straight-line quilting, use your walking foot (if you have one) as it feeds the layers evenly through your machine which helps to prevent the fabrics shifting. Use a longer stitch length than usual. If you wish, you can pay a long-arm quilter to do the quilting for you. They are able to stitch designs it is difficult to achieve on a domestic machine. Often you can see samples, and you will be able to discuss your requirements with them before they begin.

Alternatively, you can hand quilt your projects. Although this is slower than quilting by machine, it gives even more of a handmade feel and creates a beautiful finish.

In some projects you will be quilting through just the top and the wadding, but the process is just the same.

## SQUARING-UP

When the quilting is complete, you will need to square-up your quilt in preparation for binding.

1   Place a large square quilting ruler on one corner and, using the markings on the ruler to guide you, straighten up the edges so the corner is square, removing the excess backing and wadding at the same time. Make sure you leave a ¼in seam allowance on both edges. Repeat for the other corners.

2   Straighten up each edge using a longer quilting ruler, such as a 6 x 24in ruler.

## BINDING

Binding covers the raw edges of the quilt sandwich. It can match or contrast with the quilt top, and be wide or narrow, depending on the effect you want. All of the binding in this book is double-fold binding, made from 2½in wide (or 2¼in wide, if you prefer) strips of fabric – requirements are given with each project.

1   Take your binding strips and join into one long strip with 45-degree seams. Trim to ¼in seam allowances. Press the seams open to reduce bulk and trim away the 'dog-ears'.

2   Fold the strip in half lengthwise, wrong sides together, and press.

3   Working from the right side of the quilt and starting part way along one edge – I like to start at the centre of the bottom edge – match the raw edges of the binding to the raw edges of the quilt, leaving an approximately 4in long tail at the start.

4   Sew in place. When you approach a corner, stop ¼in away from the corner with the needle down. Pivot the quilt so you can sew to the corner of the quilt at a 45-degree angle, then cut the thread. This will help you achieve perfectly mitred corners. Fold the binding up over the seam you have just sewn, which will create a diagonal fold. Then fold the binding down along the next edge of the quilt. Finger press the fold you have created. Sew down the next edge. Repeat at each corner.

**5** When you get to approximately 10in from where you began sewing, stop. Take the tail of the binding that you left unsewn at the start. Straighten it up along the edge of the quilt and then fold it back on itself by 2½in. Take the remaining binding from where you stopped sewing and line up this tail with the edge of the quilt. Fold the binding back on itself leaving a ¼in gap between it and the binding you have already folded back. Finger press and cut off the excess binding from each tail.

**6** Open out both unsewn ends of binding and place them right sides together at 90 degrees and join with a 45-degree seam. Trim to ¼in seam allowance and finger press the seam open.

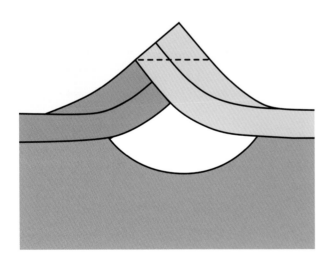

**7** Re-fold the binding wrong sides together and match up with the raw edge of the quilt. Sew in place.

**8** Fold the binding over to the back of the quilt and neatly slipstitch in place by hand.

# TEMPLATES

Templates are shown at actual size. You can download printable versions of these templates from **www.davidandcharles.com**.

## SPINNING SPECTRUM

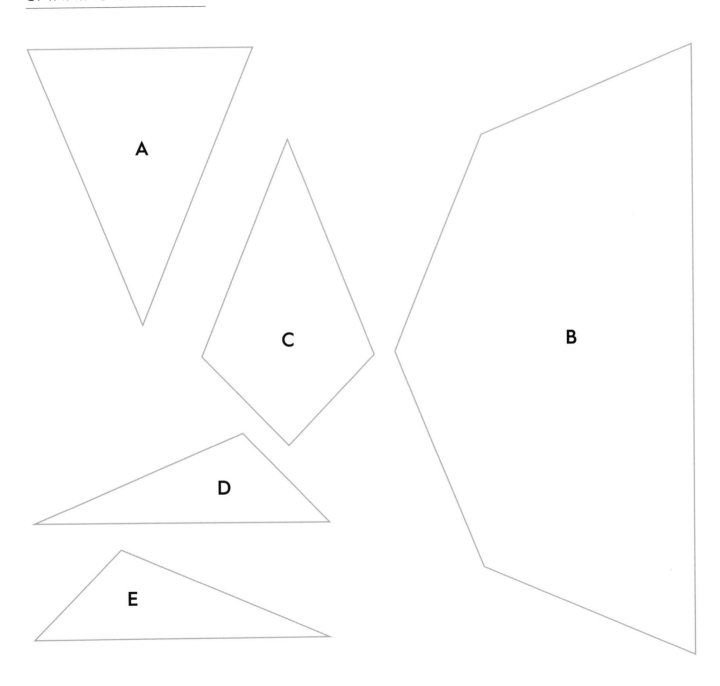

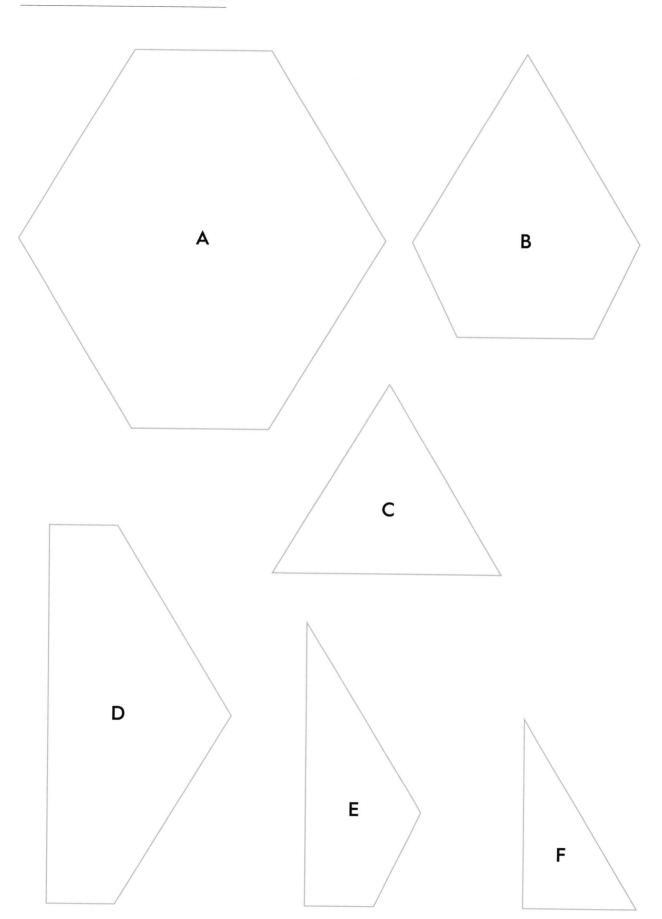

# SALT AND PEPPER

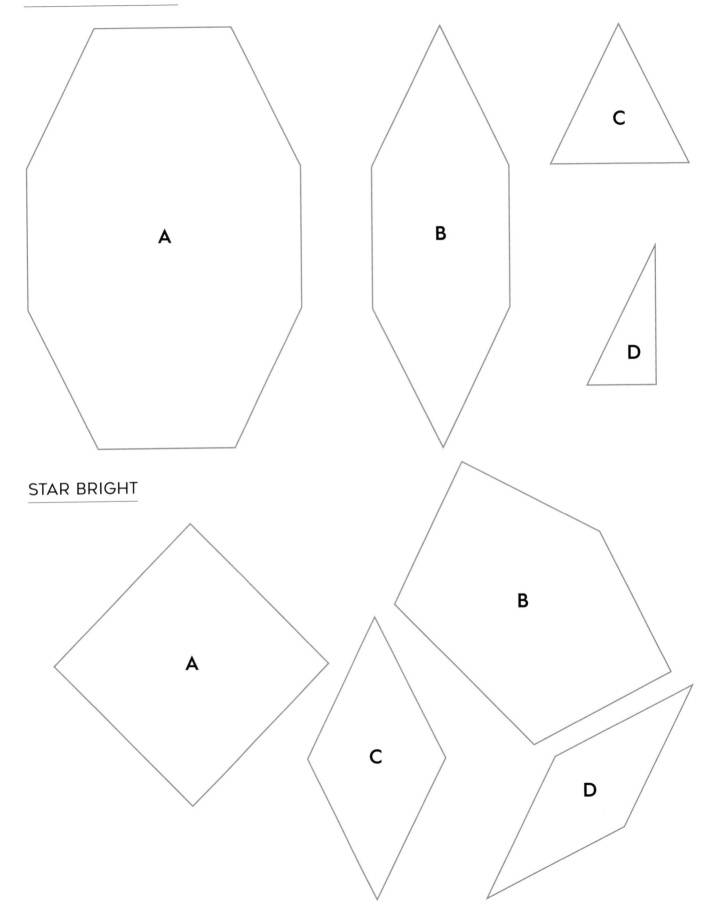

A

B

C

D

# STAR BRIGHT

A

B

C

D

# CUPCAKE FRINGE

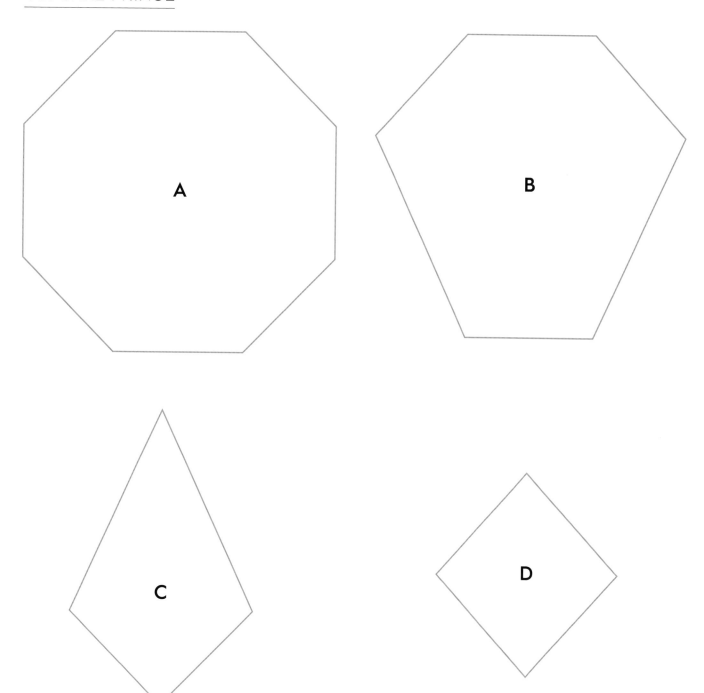

# CELTIC KNOTS

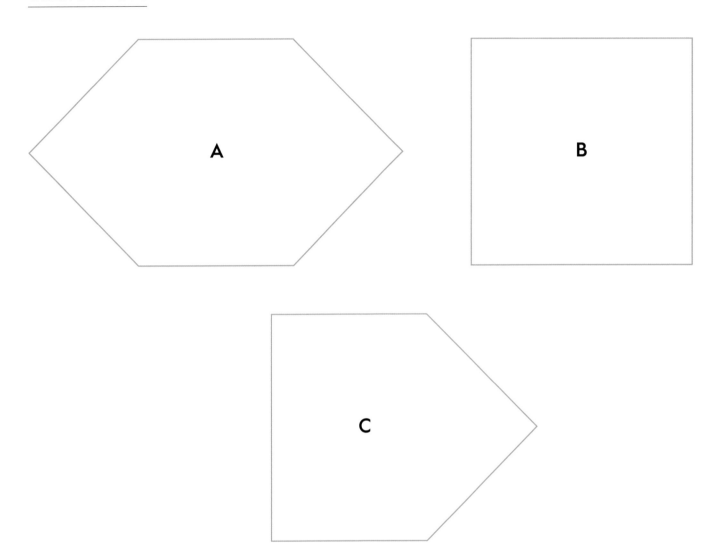

# KALEIDOSCOPE KISSES

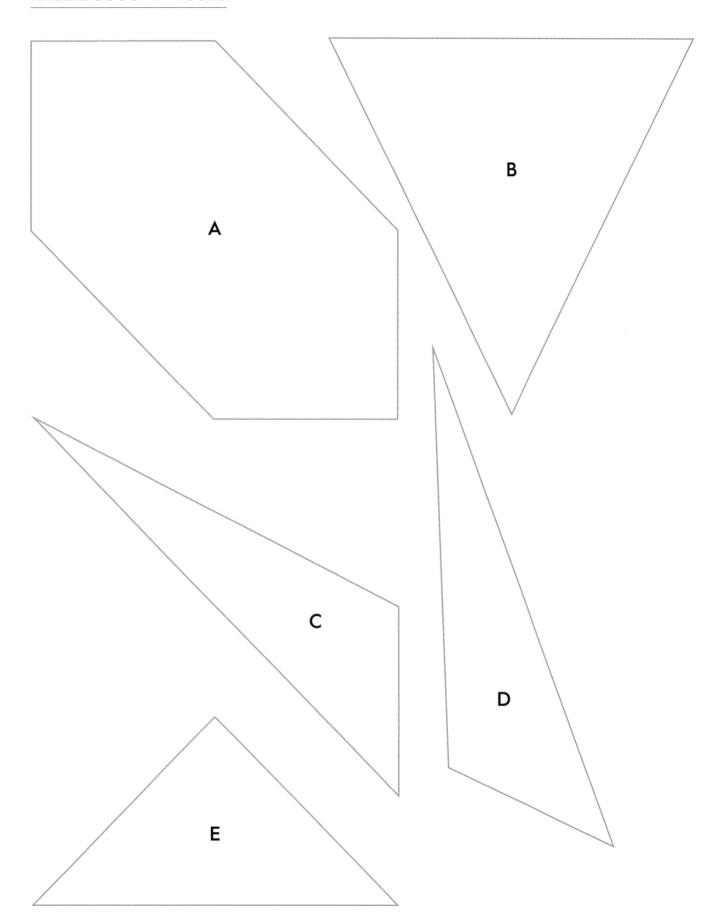

# FLOWER POWER

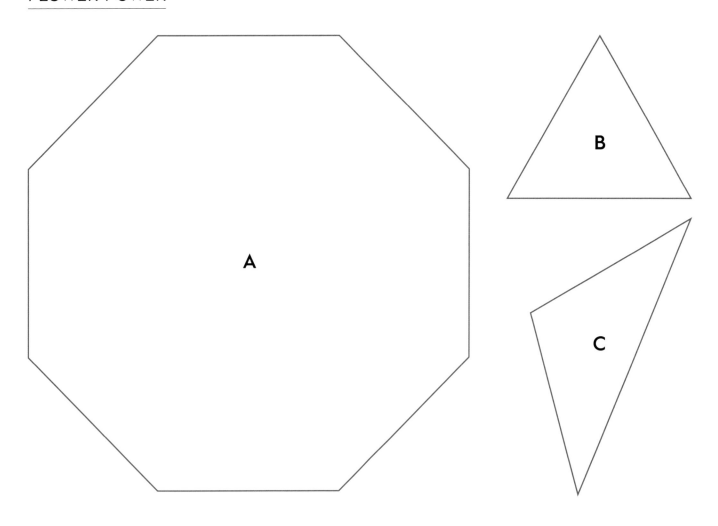

## OCEAN CIRCLE

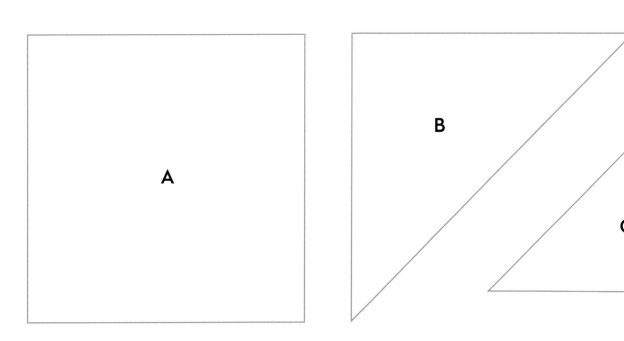

# COLOURFUL CROSSES

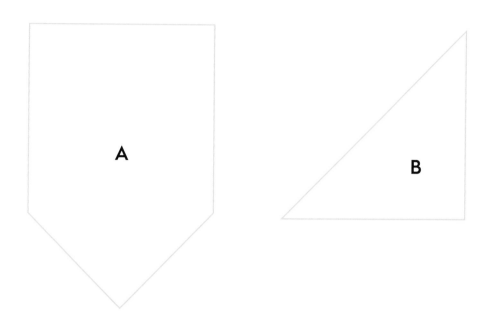

# IT'S ALL ABOUT THE HEXIES

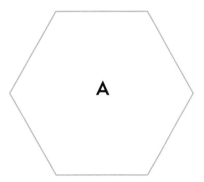

# COLOUR POP

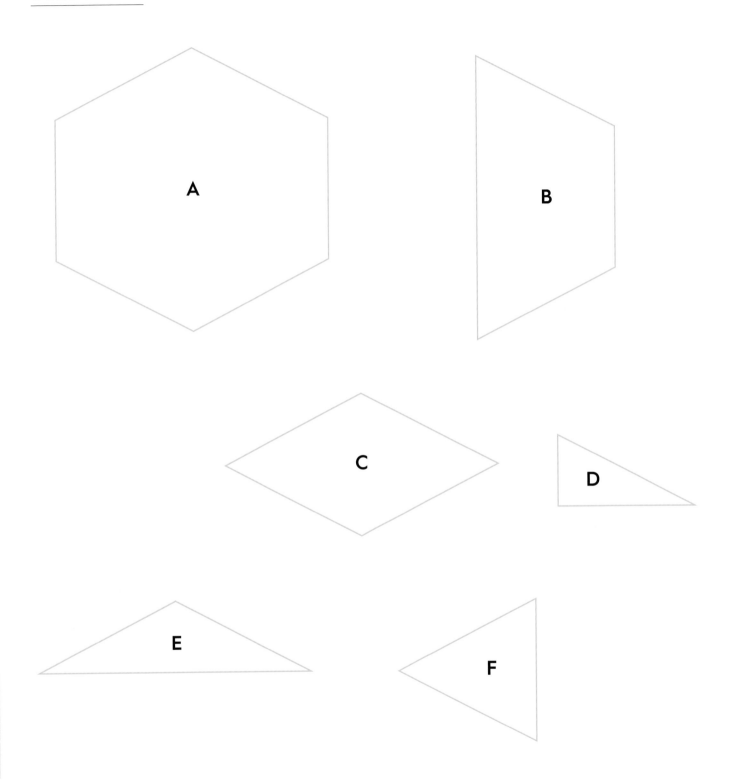

# DROPLETS BUCKET

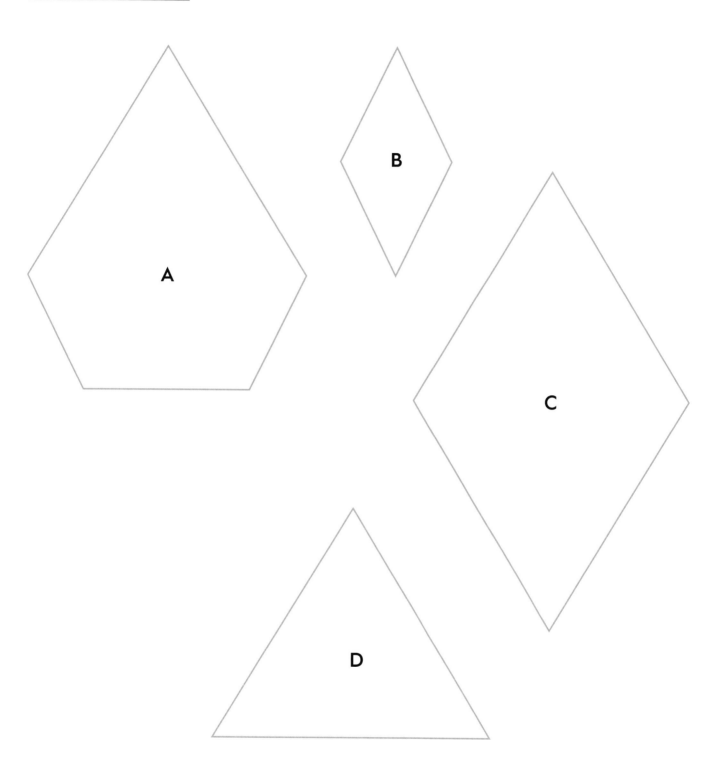

A

B

C

D

# RAINBOW STARS

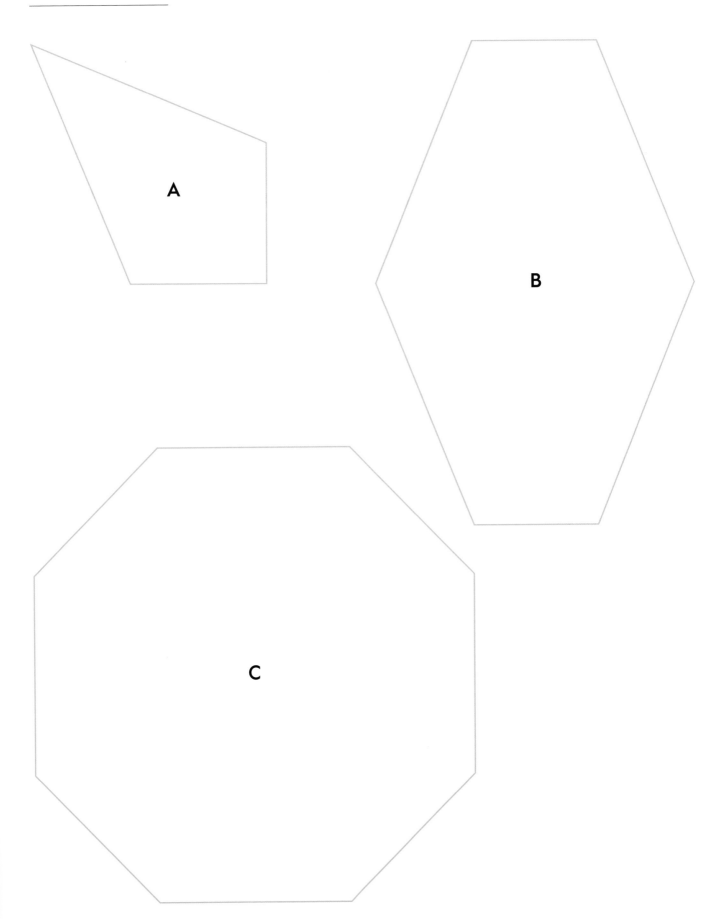

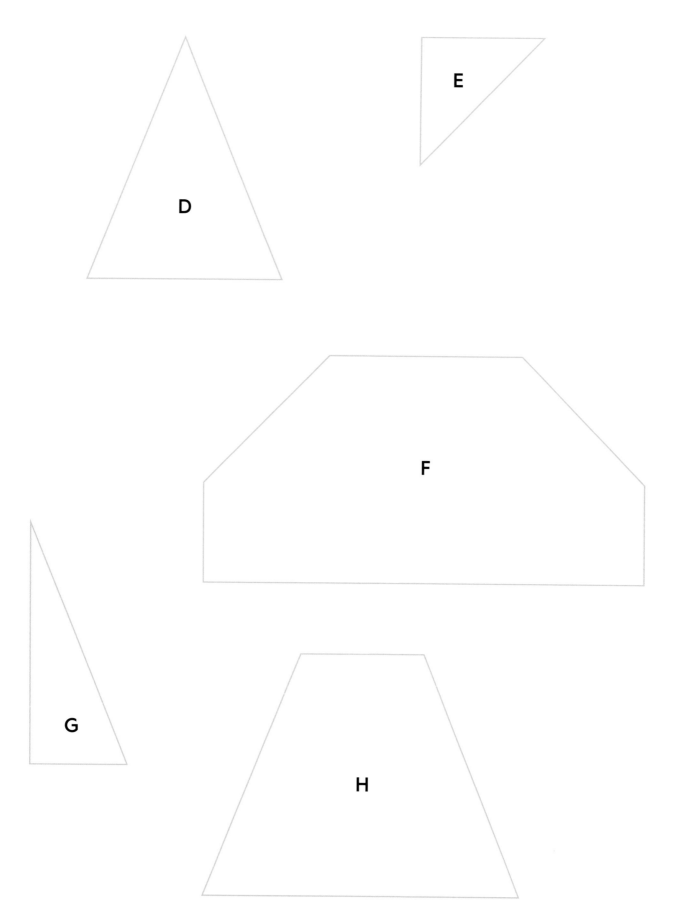

# TUMBLING WHEELS

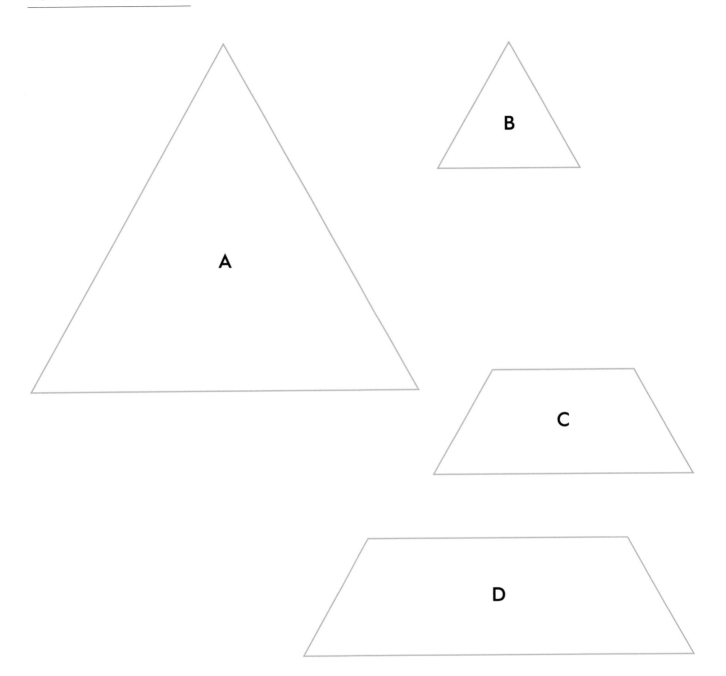

A

B

C

D

# COMFY CUBE

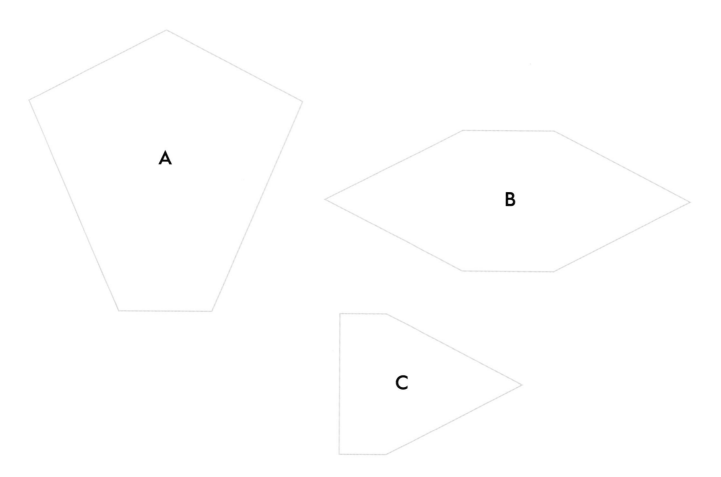

# STAR FOR A STAR

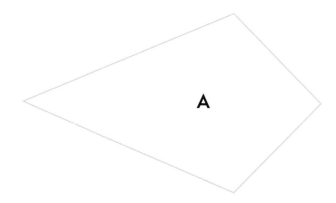

# ABOUT THE AUTHOR

Jenny has been creative from a young age and was always drawing, painting or doing cross stitch with her mum. This led her to studying Fashion and Textiles with Business Studies at the University of Brighton, where she gained a BA(Hons) specialising in Knitwear. Shortly after graduating, her son Dylan was born and she focused on raising him. Once he started school, Jenny felt the itch to be creative again and her Auntie Neets invited her to stay for a weekend of quilting. That was it, she was hooked! Realising a sewing machine was too loud to use in the evenings, Jenny was on a mission to find a quieter alternative. She discovered English Paper Piecing (EPP) and has never looked back. Within a few months she was designing her own patterns, followed by writing and designing for magazines, countless television appearances demonstrating EPP and quilting, as well as selling her patterns, paper pieces and kits via her website.

**www.hashtagsew.com**

## ACKNOWLEDGEMENTS

A massive special thanks to my family. Without the constant love and support of my mum and dad none of this would be possible. To my friends for their cheerleading along the way. And to my son Dylan, the most amazing, caring and understanding boy who makes me proud every single day, keep being you.

I would also like to thank the incredible team at David and Charles for giving me this fantastic opportunity. My publisher Sarah Callard has been unstintingly encouraging all the way through, and project editor Anne Williams is a gem who has made the whole process stress-free.

A humongous thank you, too, to my friend and long-arm quilter Hannah Bradley-Cohen for working her magic on the long-arm quilted pieces in the book. Also to Lisa Lam who has given me endless advice, kept me calm and made me laugh till my sides hurt. And last but not least, thank you to the awesome sewing community for supporting my business and for the endless online giggles and chats – you are truly special.

## SUPPLIERS

Thank you to:

- The fabulous designer Alison Glass, for arranging to have her Art Theory Fabrics designs sent to me to use throughout the book. **www.alisonglass.com**

- Makower UK, for providing me with all the Spectrum solids and Linen Texture colours I needed to complement the prints. **www.makoweruk.com**

- Creative Grids, for sending me some brand-new rulers in all different sizes. I am so grateful – these have been used non-stop. **www.creativegrids.com**

- Aurifil Threads, for letting me choose all the different coloured and weight threads I wanted, you have been so kind. **www.aurifil.com**

- EQS, for sending me endless Sewline glue refills – you know how many I get through! **www.eqsuk.com**

- Hannah Bradley-Cohen, for long-arm quilting some of the projects in the book. **www.thebespokequilter.com**

- Franklins, for sewing supplies. **www.franklinsgroup.com**

- Juki sewing machines and servicing. **www.jukiuk.com**

# INDEX

A DAVID AND CHARLES BOOK
© David and Charles, Ltd 2022

David and Charles is an imprint of David and Charles, Ltd
Suite A, Tourism House, Pynes Hill, Exeter, EX2 5WS

Text and Designs © Jenny Jackson 2022
Layout and Photography © David and Charles, Ltd 2022

First published in the UK and USA in 2022

A catalogue record for this book is available from the
British Library.

ISBN-13: 9781446309049 paperback
ISBN-13: 9781446381366 EPUB
ISBN-13: 9781446381359 PDF

This book has been printed on paper from approved
suppliers and made from pulp from sustainable sources.

Printed in the UK by Buxton Press for:
David and Charles, Ltd
Suite A, Tourism House, Pynes Hill, Exeter, EX2 5WS

10 9 8 7 6 5 4 3 2

Publishing Director: Ame Verso
Senior Commissioning Editor: Sarah Callard
Managing Editor: Jeni Chown
Project Editor: Anne Williams
Head of Design: Sam Staddon
Designers: Lucy Waldron and Blanche Williams
Pre-press Designer: Ali Stark
Illustrations: Kuo Kang Chen
Art Direction: Prudence Rogers
Photography: Jason Jenkins
Production Manager: Beverley Richardson

David and Charles publishes high-quality books on
a wide range of subjects. For more information visit
www.davidandcharles.com.

Share your makes with us on social media using
#dandcbooks and follow us on Facebook and Instagram
by searching for @dandcbooks.

Layout of the digital edition of this book may vary
depending on reader hardware and display settings.